"*Psychological Perspectives on Radicalization* is a must read for researchers, policy makers, and lay people alike looking for a sophisticated understanding of the pathways to radicalization and deradicalization. It provides a novel social psychological analysis of the phenomenon by integrating micro, meso, and macro-level processes thereby advancing our knowledge of the when, why, and how individuals radicalize."

Jolanda Jetten, ARC Laureate Fellow, Professor of Social Psychology,
FASSA, School of Psychology, University of Queensland, Australia

"This primer to radicalization summarizes the latest results from academic research in an easy to understand way, without over-simplifying a complex phenomenon. Beyond that, the authors of this volume offer an original model of radicalization of their own and also break new ground in their discussion of resilience to radicalization and, paradoxically, to deradicalization."

Prof. Em. Alex P. Schmid, Editor-in-Chief, "Perspectives on Terrorism,"
and former Officer-in-Charge of the United Nations'
Terrorism Prevention Branch at UNODC

"This very well organized and clearly written volume should be studied by everyone interested to better understand radicalization, from introductory students to advanced experts. The authors have produced a highly valuable contribution to our understanding of radicalization."

Fathali M. Moghaddam, Professor and Director of the Interdisciplinary
Program in Cognitive Science, Georgetown University, U.S.

"This book is the perfect introduction kit for anyone who wants to start, do, or reflect on terrorism and radicalization research. It has all the necessary components: key questions on the why, how, and end of terrorism, a serious chapter on methodologies, but it also contains crucial criticisms on far-too-easy one-dimensional radicalization models. In order to understand, make, and solve the radicalization puzzle, reading this book gives every student and researcher a head start."

Beatrice de Graaf, Professor of History of International Relations and
Global Governance, Strategic Theme Institutions for Open Societies,
Department for History and Art History,
Utrecht University, The Netherlands

"Applying a psychological perspective, the authors make a valuable effort to establish factors that explain why some individuals adopt beliefs that violence is a justifiable and necessary means to achieve changes in society, and what characterize those that take the step from beliefs into action."

Dr. Tore Bjørgo, Professor at the University of Oslo
and the Norwegian Police University College,
Director of Center for Research on Extremism (C-REX), Norway

"Solid and well-reasoned reappraisal of one of the oldest issues in the study of terrorism: how do psychological processes influence individuals and groups to embrace political violence? A must-read, written by a highly qualified team of researchers."

Rik Coolsaet, Professor Emeritus, Ghent University, Belgium

Psychological Perspectives on Radicalization

This innovative book examines radicalization from new psychological perspectives by examining the different typologies of radicalizing individuals, what makes individuals resilient against radicalization, and events that can trigger individuals to radicalize or to deradicalize.

What is radicalization? Which psychological processes or events in a person's life play a role in radicalization? What determines whether a person is resilient against radicalization, and is deradicalization something that we can achieve? This book goes beyond previous publications on this topic by identifying concrete key events in the process of radicalization, providing a useful theoretical framework that summarizes the current state-of-the-art research on radicalization and deradicalization. A model is presented in which a distinction is made between different levels of radicalization and deradicalization, with key underlying psychological needs discussed: the need for identity, justice, significance, and sensation. The authors also describe what makes people resilient against messages from "the outside world" when they belong to an extremist group and discusses observable events which may "trigger" a person to radicalize (further) or to deradicalize.

Including real-world examples and clear guidelines for interventions aimed at prevention of radicalization and stimulation of deradicalization, this is essential reading for policy makers, researchers, practitioners, and students interested in this crucial societal issue.

Dr. Allard R. Feddes received his PhD at the Friedrich-Schiller University of Jena, Germany, in 2007, on development of prejudice in childhood. He now is assistant professor in the Social Psychology Department at the University of Amsterdam. He is interested in how group membership influences our feelings, thoughts, and behavior and has studied the psychology of (de)radicalization since 2011.

Lars Nickolson graduated cum laude as a Master in Philosophy in 2008. For more than a decade, he has been involved with counter-radicalization policy both as a researcher and an advisor, working within and outside of the Dutch government. He is currently a PhD candidate at the Department of Political Science at the University of Amsterdam.

Dr. Liesbeth Mann obtained her PhD at the University of Amsterdam studying the emotion of humiliation in interpersonal and intergroup contexts. Currently, she works at the same university as a teacher and researcher in cultural and political psychology. She is also involved in a number of (governmental) projects focused on the process of (de)radicalization.

Dr. Bertjan Doosje was Professor of Radicalization in the Department of Social Psychology at the University of Amsterdam from 2013 until 2019 and is currently Associate Professor there. He received his PhD on stereotyping in intergroup contexts in 1995 (cum laude). Since then, he has examined intergroup relations in general, and after 9/11/2001, he has developed a special focus on radicalization and terrorism.

Psychological Perspectives on Radicalization

Allard R. Feddes, Lars Nickolson, Liesbeth Mann, and Bertjan Doosje

LONDON AND NEW YORK

First published 2020
by Routledge
2 Park Square, Milton Park, Abingdon, Oxon OX14 4RN

and by Routledge
52 Vanderbilt Avenue, New York, NY 10017

Routledge is an imprint of the Taylor & Francis Group, an informa business

© 2020 Allard R. Feddes, Lars Nickolson, Liesbeth Mann, and Bertjan Doosje

British Library Cataloguing-in-Publication Data
A catalogue record for this book is available from the British Library

Library of Congress Cataloging-in-Publication Data
A catalog record has been requested for this book

ISBN: 978-1-138-89756-4 (hbk)
ISBN: 978-1-138-89757-1 (pbk)
ISBN: 978-1-315-17883-7 (ebk)

Typeset in Perpetua
by Nova Techset Private Limited, Bengaluru & Chennai, India

Contents

Theoretical model

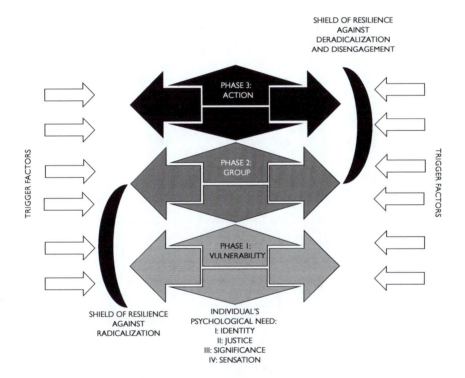

Model of radicalization, deradicalization, and disengagement. (Reprinted from *Current Opinion in Psychology*, 11, Doosje, B., Moghaddam, F. M., Kruglanski, A. W., De Wolf, A., Mann, L., & Feddes, A. R., Terrorism, radicalization and de-radicalization, 79–84, Copyright 2016, with permission from Elsevier.)

Foreword

Why do people join or support extremist groups? Why are people willing to use violence to change society? Often, a process of radicalization precedes this violence. Much has been written about processes of radicalization. The aim of this book is to summarize the state of the art of research on radicalization and de-radicalization. We aim for a wide audience, including students, researchers, policy makers, first-line workers, and teachers. In this book, we have tried to use an informal writing style limiting academic jargon. We hope that this book will thereby reach both those who are starting to explore this research field and those who are already familiar with it.

We would like to extend our sincere thanks to our editors at Routledge, Eleanor Reedy and Alex Howard, for their support and advice over the past three years. We would also like to thank our copy-editor Ellie Fountain for thoroughly going through the text, and we owe our thanks to Narayani Govindarajan, Project Manager, and her team at Nova Techset for their support on this project.

Allard R. Feddes
Lars Nickolson
Liesbeth Mann
Bertjan Doosje
Amsterdam/Berlin, April 3 2020

Chapter 1

Introduction

Goals

- Present two concrete examples of members from two different radical groups.
- Outline why radicalization is an important topic to study.
- Give a brief historical overview of terrorism.
- Present the scope and outline of this book.

Introduction

Mohammed Bouyeri (see Box 1.1) was 26 years old when he assassinated the Dutch filmmaker Theo van Gogh on November 2, 2004, in Amsterdam, The Netherlands. The Dutch-Moroccan Bouyeri was part of a small group (The Hofstad group) of youngsters with radical ideas. What made him decide to murder Theo van Gogh?

Anders Breivik (see Box 1.2) was 32 years old when he committed two deadly attacks in Norway on July 22, 2011. First, he planted a bomb in a car next to a government building in Oslo, killing eight people. Second, two hours later, he murdered 69 youngsters from a socialist background who were enjoying a summer camp on the island Utøya, 50 kilometers from Oslo. Why did he do this?

These are just two examples of people deciding to commit acts of terror by murdering other people. Why? What could have been their motives? What did they aim to achieve? In this book, we aim to provide answers to these questions by drawing on scientific theories and empirical research on radicalization and terrorism. In doing so, we mostly (but not exclusively) draw on literature from a psychological perspective. We will find out that there is no simple checklist to determine why, when, and how a person might execute a terror attack. Still, we argue it is possible to establish certain factors that increase the likelihood that a person might believe violence is a valid and necessary tool to achieve changes in a society. In Boxes 1.1 and 1.2, we describe the lives of Mohammed Bouyeri and Anders Breivik, respectively. In subsequent chapters, we will draw on these examples to illustrate certain issues or arguments we present.

Box 1.1   Mohammed Bouyeri

- Born on March 8, 1978.
- Assassinated Dutch filmmaker Theo van Gogh on November 2, 2004, in Amsterdam, The Netherlands.
- Convicted of murder on July 26, 2005, Bouyeri received a life sentence without a chance of parole.

On March 8, 1978, Mohammed Bouyeri is born in (the Eastern part of) Amsterdam, The Netherlands. When he turns 7, Bouyeri moves to an area in the West of Amsterdam (Slotervaart/Overtoomse Veld). Aged 12, Bouyeri goes to second highest level of secondary school (Havo) at the Mondriaan Lyceum. "He was timid and attentive," according to a teacher at this school (quoted in 2005 in NRC Handelsblad). "He wanted to make a career. He had to work hard to receive his degree." In 1997, Bouyeri goes to the college Hogeschool Holland in Diemen near Amsterdam. He spends five years at this college, pursuing several majors. He does not complete any of them.

In 2000, Bouyeri is involved in a violent incident for the first time. At the campus bar of Hogeschool Holland, he and his friends challenge Dutch students, and there is a fight. In 2001, he and another young Dutch person with a Moroccan background start a fight over Bouyeri's younger sister. When the police arrive, Bouyeri shows his knife and tries to cut an agent. Finally, he throws the knife at the head of the agent. For this violent incident, Bouyeri serves a prison sentence.

He is released at the end of 2001. This is a period in which his mother dies and the attacks on the Twin Towers take place. Bouyeri starts at the Higher College Amsterdam with the major social pedagogical caregiving. He also becomes active at the local youth center, Eigenwijks, helping youth in his neighborhood, Slotervaart/Overtoomse Veld.

In 2002, he starts taking action to try to create his own place for the youth at the high school Mondriaan Lyceum where they can do their homework and relax. However, his plan is not accepted by the authorities. According to Wim Knol, owner of the youth center Eigenwijks, Bouyeri is disappointed. He quotes Bouyeri: "I have had enough of the institutions," and "We Moroccan people are good enough to be used as a contact person, as long as we do not take initiatives."

His appearance changes: he starts wearing a beard and traditional clothing, including a djellaba (long, loose-fitting robe with long sleeves and often a kind of hood; it is worn down to the ankles and usually has a neutral color). He decides to stop with his college and education at the end of 2002 (Figure 1.1).

After the summer of 2003, Bouyeri changes dramatically. He starts religious arguments with people from the local youth center, Eigenwijks (he does not want to serve alcohol, and he wants separate rooms for men and women). From then on, people from Eigenwijks start to lose sight of Bouyeri. He also no longer wants to interact with the Moroccan youth in his neighborhood. He starts to dislike their hanging around and their use of soft drugs and alcohol. In addition, he distances himself from his family. At first, he wants to convert his family to his notion of the true Islam. However, when he fails to do so, there seems to be more distance between him and his family. Finally, he also stops going to the local Moroccan mosque, El Ouma, where his father prays every Friday. Apparently, he tells the Imam: "You do not tell the truth." He now goes to the Salafi mosque, El Tawheed, in a nearby area, Oud-West. He interacts with a Syrian man named Abu Khaled, a Jihadi advocate, who teaches him more anti-Western attitudes.

Bouyeri starts articulating his ideas on paper and in discussions. For example, he is quoted as disliking national sentiments (both Moroccan and

Figure 1.1 Mohammed Bouyeri in 2004. (From https://en.wikipedia.org/wiki/Mohammed_Bouyeri.)

Dutch): "The strongest bond is thus the religious bond. This bond is stronger than the stupid nationalistic and chauvinistic sentiments, as well as relations based on blood ancestry" (quoted in Bahara, 2014). His dislike for the Dutch legal system is illustrated by this quote: "Authorities of 'kuffaar' (infidels) over Muslims are not valid." Finally, he writes to the youth: "Liberate yourself! Get out of that coffee shop, get out that bar, get out of that corner. Join the caravan of Martyrs. Rise up from your deep sleep, rise up and shake the dust of humiliation off of you. Rise up and listen to the call HAJJA AL JIHAD" (quoted in Bahara, 2014).

On November 2, 2004, Bouyeri shoots the Dutch filmmaker and Islam critic Theo van Gogh, who is cycling on the streets of Amsterdam. Van Gogh falls from his bicycle and pleads: "Mercy. Mercy. We can still talk about it." But Bouyeri shoots again, this time killing him, and leaves a farewell note, as he expects to die in the following moments during his arrest. But he is arrested alive in a park nearby.

On the second and final day of his trial, Bouyeri says, "I have let myself be led by the rule that commands me to chop off the head of everyone that insults Allah and the prophet." And to the mother of Van Gogh, he says: "I must admit that I do not empathize. I do not feel your pain. I cannot. I do not know what it is like to lose a child that you have brought to the world with so much pain and tears. This is partly due to the fact that I am not a woman. And partly I cannot empathize with you because you are an infidel."

Mohammed Bouyeri is convicted of murder on July 26, 2005. He receives a life sentence without a chance of parole.

In 2006, Bouyeri has to appear in court again, this time for his involvement in the Hofstad group, the group of radicalized/extremist people around him. The court finds him guilty of being the leader of this group. This does not translate into a longer sentence, as he has already received the maximum (i.e., life) sentence.

Sources used in this box:

Bahara, H. (2014). "Rijst op uit jullie slaap" ['Rise from your sleep']. De Groene Amsterdammer, October 22. https://www.groene.nl/artikel/rijst-op-uit-jullie-slaap.

Buijs, F. J., Demant, F., & Hamdy, A. (2006). *Warriors from own soil: Radical and democratic Muslims in The Netherlands*. Amsterdam: Amsterdam University Press.

Wikipedia entry on Mohammed Bouyeri. https://en.wikipedia.org/wiki/Mohammed_Bouyeri.

Box 1.2 Anders (Behring) Breivik

- Born on February 13, 1979.
- On July 22, 2011, Breivik killed eight people with a car bomb in Oslo, Norway. A couple of hours later, with guns and dressed as a policeman, he murdered 69 youngsters associated with the youth organisation of the Labour Party, on the small island Utøya, 50 kilometers from Oslo.
- Convicted of murder on August 24, 2012, Breivik received the maximum prison sentence in Norway, which is 21 years, with a minimum of 10 years.

Anders Behring Breivik is born in Oslo, Norway, on February 13, 1979. His parents divorce when Breivik is one year old, and he lives with his mother in Oslo-West. His father first lives in London and later in France. Both his parents remarry.

During Breivik's early childhood, his mother hits him and can be cold to him. Two reports (by psychologists) on Breivik's weak mental health appear when he is just four years old. Breivik regularly visits his father and stepmother in France until he is 14. His contact with his father ends when Breivik is 16 years old, either because of the father (according to the mother's version) or because of Breivik (according to the father's version).

When he is between 12 and 15 years old, Breivik is part of the hip hop community. He shows a great interest in graffiti. Perhaps due to his fanaticism, he gets caught by the police several times. Breivik is confirmed into the Lutheran Church of Norway at the age of 15, but is never very fanatic in his religion (Figure 1.2).

In addition, Breivik starts to show a great interest in his physical appearance. This is evidenced by his heavy weight training, his use of anabolic steroids, and the fact that he undergoes plastic surgery (chin, nose, and forehead). He helps children/students who get bullied.

In his 20s, he tries a political career in the right-wing populist party 'Fremskrittspartiet' for the local elections of Oslo-West. He is seriously hurt when he finds out that the local party organisation did not put him as a candidate on their electoral list for the municipality election.

Breivik earns money via shady businesses, such as producing fake degree certificates, but has to stop when he is about to be uncovered. According to Breivik himself, he also loses money in the stock market.

In his personal life, some friends claim that he suffers quite a bit from a failed romance. According to a friend, Breivik changes after being dumped by a Belarusian girl he met via the internet.

Possibly due to poor financial circumstances, Breivik moves back into his mother's apartment in Oslo-West when he is 28. He spends four to five

Figure 1.2 Sketch of Anders Behring Breivik. (From https://en.wikipedia.org/wiki/
Anders_Behring_Breivik.)

years there without much employment and playing a great deal of violent video games.

He clearly shows an interest in weapons. As a member of a pistol club in Oslo, he is able to buy a pistol legally, as well as a semi-automatic rifle by possessing a hunting license.

In 2011, he moves out of Oslo "to become a farmer" in a remote area, while in reality planning the attack in Oslo with the chemical materials (e.g., fertilizers) he is able to order as a farmer. He tests explosives. His friends try to visit him, but he keeps them away.

He carefully plans the attacks in Oslo and on the island Utøya on July 22, 2011. For example, he puts a sign indicating "Sorry: sewage works" in the window of the rented van he uses for the Oslo attack, because he is afraid the smell of the chemicals inside the van might alert people. With a car bomb, he first kills eight people in Oslo. He then drives about 50 kilometers to the north. With guns and dressed as a policeman, he persuades the ferryman to bring him over small island Utøya, and that he is a policeman sent to guard the safety of the people on the island in the aftermath of the events in Oslo. Once on the island, he first kills the camp director and an off-duty policeman. Subsequently, it takes him more than one hour to kill 69 people in total, most of them young people associated with the socialist party trapped on the small island, shouting, "You are going to die today, Marxists!"

When counter-terrorism police arrive on the island, Breivik surrenders without resistance. He confesses and indicates that the attacks have been planned to save Norway and Western Europe from a Muslim invasion. In his view, the Labour Party has been responsible for allowing this invasion to happen.

Breivik leaves a 1516-page manifesto entitled: "2083: A European Declaration of Independence."

Before the trial, psychiatrists diagnose him with paranoid schizophrenia. They indicate that Breivik is psychotic when he carries out the attacks as well as during their observations. These psychiatrists find Breivik "criminally insane."

This comes as a shock to Breivik and to psychiatrists charged with observing his current behavior in his prison before the trial. Breivik has expressed the hope of being declared mentally sane. He writes about the prospect of being sent to a psychiatric hospital: "I must admit this is the worst thing that could have happened to me as it is the ultimate humiliation. To send a political activist to a mental hospital is more sadistic and evil than to kill him! It is a fate worse than death."

Fortunately for him, subsequent psychiatrists conclude that Breivik has *not* been psychotic during the attacks, nor during their evaluations. They do diagnose him with an antisocial personality disorder and a narcissistic personality disorder. This means Breivik can be sent to prison, but not to a mental hospital.

Convicted of murder on August 24, 2012, Breivik receives the maximum prison sentence in Norway, which is 21 years, with a minimum of 10 years.

Sources used for this box:

The Guardian, July 23, 2011. Article by Norwegian writer Karl Ove Knausgaard. https://www.theguardian.com/world/2011/jul/23/anders-behring-breivik-norway-attacks.

The Telegraph, July 22, 2016. https://www.telegraph.co.uk/news/2016/07/22/anders-breivik-inside-the-warped-mind-of-a-mass-killer/.

Wikipedia entry on Anders Behring Breivik. https://en.wikipedia.org/wiki/Anders_Behring_Breivik.

Wikipedia entry on 2011 Norway attacks. https://en.wikipedia.org/wiki/2011_Norway_attacks.

At the start of this book on p. ix, our theoretical model of radicalization, deradicalization, and disengagement is presented. As a starting point, we make a distinction between three general phases of radicalization: the vulnerability phase, the group phase, and the action phase. In addition, two shields of resilience are distinguished: the shield of resilience against radicalization and, once an individual is a member of an extremist group, the shield of resilience to deradicalize and disengage from the extremist scene. In the model, we also focus on four psychological needs that can make a person vulnerable to radicalization: the need for identity, the need for justice, the need for significance, and the need for sensation. Finally, the model shows that trigger factors play a role in each phase of radicalization. As we will see, trigger factors can also help us explain why individuals radicalize or deradicalize from one phase to another. Finally, as can be seen, individuals can radicalize (move up in the model) or deradicalize (move down in the model), but individuals may also move horizontally (for example, when an individual leaves one extremist group and joins another). Throughout this book, we will discuss in more depth the different elements of this model.

Why is studying radicalization important?

Terrorism is an important security issue in our times, as it has been historically. For example, in the 60s/70s of the last century, in Europe alone, there were the Rote Armee Fraktion (RAF) in Germany, the Red Brigade in Italy, the Irish Republican Army (IRA) in the Great Britain, and the Euskadi Ta Askatasuna (ETA) in the Basque regions in Spain and France. They were responsible for terrorist attacks leading to thousands of deaths. Similarly, presently, we are confronted with a great number of terrorist attacks around the world, resulting in many deaths, almost on a daily basis.

From Figure 1.3, we can see that, worldwide, terrorism has increased steadily from around 1970, with a more pronounced rise after 2000 and again a rise after 2011. This means terrorism is not just historic, but very much an important current issue.

Figure 1.4 indicates both the number of people killed in terrorist attacks as well as the number of attacks in Europe from 1970 to 2017. From this figure, we can conclude that the 70s, 80s, and early 90s were particularly violent. Subsequently, after '95, it became less violent, but there were serious incidents in Madrid and Norway (Oslo/Utøya – see Box 1.2). Finally, starting from 2015, Europe has suffered from several attacks again in several countries (twice in Paris, France and in Brussels, Belgium; Nice, France; London, England; and Berlin, Germany).

However, it is important to note that strictly speaking in terms of numbers of casualties, terrorism may *not* be considered that important. For example, on average, there are many more deaths due to traffic accidents than due to terrorism. However, terrorism has important psychological consequences as well. Victims or bystanders of terrorist attacks often experience fear and anger after such attacks, and they can suffer from post-traumatic stress disorder (PTSD) symptoms, including intrusive thoughts and emotions, panic attacks, and impaired sleep, resulting in loss of productivity (Schuster et al., 2001; DiGrande et al., 2008).

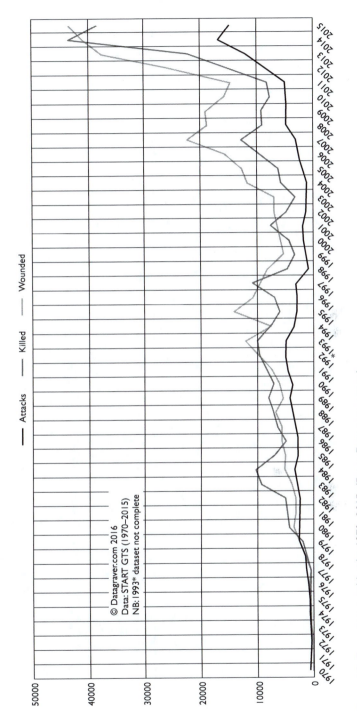

Figure 1.3 Terrorism worldwide, 1970–2015. (From Datagraver.com.)

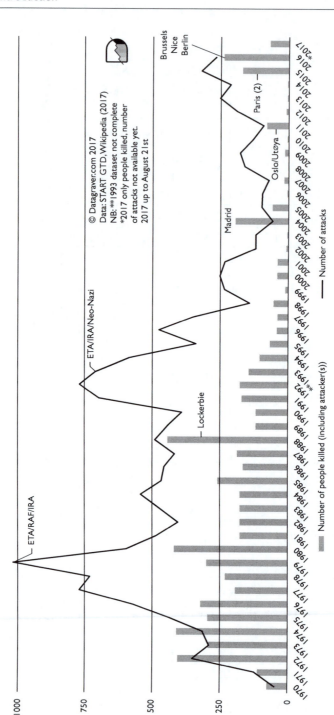

Figure 1.4 Terrorism in Western Europe 1970–2017. (From Datagraver.com.)

Furthermore, terrorism has serious psychological and political implications at the group or societal level. The most dramatic effect is that it can create polarization and tensions in society. For example, to the extent that non-Islamic people blame all Islamic people for producing "Islamic terrorists" (Doosje, Zebel, Scheermeier, & Mathyi, 2007), it creates divisions between people along religious lines in European countries. Similarly, perceived threat due to terrorism is associated with more discrimination against Muslims (above and beyond the association between blatant and subtle forms of prejudice and discrimination; Doosje, Zimmermann, Küpper, Zick, & Meertens, 2010). Indeed, some right-wing political parties in Europe have been able to propagate their ideas due to feelings of fear and anger among a broader population due to terrorism in Europe. This results in further polarization between different groups in society.

At the same time, often in the direct aftermath of terrorist attacks, political changes have been instigated, including more thorough security checks at airports and more legal possibilities for intelligence services to gather (online) information on potential terrorists. For some people, such measures may provide them with a greater feeling of safety, but for other people, these measures can undermine a sense of privacy.

Some of these consequences are in line with the goals that the terrorist group aims to achieve via violence. First, terrorism is meant to persuade other people of the importance of the main concerns of the terrorist group. For example, violent actions against abortion doctors may make other people aware that the fact that these abortions take place is a serious concern for their group. In addition, with these actions, terrorists often aim to influence those people who work in a particular field to try to make them reconsider the work that they are doing. In our example, these actions are meant to try to stop doctors from performing abortions. Finally, terrorism often aims to persuade politicians to address the issue that the terrorists deem important. Thus, in our case, the actions are meant to (directly or indirectly) influence politicians' actions with respect to abortions.

Finally, a better understanding of the psychological variables involved in radicalization and terrorism will also provide better clues on how to counter radicalization. As such, it can potentially help to reduce the incidence of radicalization and potential terrorist attacks.

To summarize, (the threat of) terrorism plays an important role in current societies. Studying radicalization from a psychological perspective is important in order to understand the process that may lead to terrorism. Consequences of terrorism include direct effects for the victims of violence (such as PTSD), often more stringent laws and regulations that aim to strengthen national security, and also more indirect effects in terms of creating (further) divisions in a society.

A brief historical overview of terrorism

In terms of the history of terrorism, it is possible to distinguish four waves (e.g., Rapoport, 2004). The first wave is labeled "the anarchist wave" (1880–1920), the second "the anti-colonial wave" (1920–1960), the third "the left wave" (1960–2000), and finally the fourth "the religious wave" (1979–present). Although one can argue about the specific choices of these waves (e.g., they are mainly Western focused), they do indicate some important points. One is that terrorism is not at all a recent phenomenon. Rather, throughout history (and before the first wave), it is possible to distinguish terrorist groups that have used violence as a means to achieve political changes and claim their goals. Second, while there is a current focus on the religious dimension of terrorism, this has clearly not always been the case.

Three points of clarification

At this point, we want to make three points clear. First, it is important to make a distinction between the role of scientists in terms of analyzing and trying to understand the reasons and motives behind certain behavior (in this case performing terrorist attacks) and justifying the actions. Specifically, we stress that our motivation to understand the reasons behind actions does not imply a motivation to justify these actions. Thus, our analysis in terms of reasons or motives does not alter the fact that illegal (violent) actions have been undertaken that cannot be justified and, as such, demand punitive legal actions no matter what the motives might have been and how well one might be able to understand them.

Second, we are fully aware that terrorism is a highly subjective, ideologically loaded term. Thus, one person's terrorist is another person's freedom fighter. In addition, this perception can change over time (e.g., the image of Nelson Mandela in the Western media has transformed from a terrorist to freedom fighter to successful president of South Africa after Apartheid). Relatedly, radicalization is a relative concept, in that some people can be radical only to the extent that other people define a point of reference. For example, in most countries, the use of violence against other people is forbidden by law (created by the majority). Consequently, the use of violence to achieve political goals is construed as radical violent behavior that should be punished. However, the same violent behavior against other people might be legitimized and supported when the majority of citizens of a country consider this violence a valid response to a security threat (e.g., invasions in other countries after having suffered from a terrorist attack by an out-group). Thus, whether an act of violence is conceived of as an act of terrorism or an act of patriotism makes it difficult, if not impossible, to create an overall conceptualization of radicalization and terrorism.

Third and relatedly, in our view, terrorism and radicalization are best conceived in terms of intergroup relations, such that oftentimes, groups in conflict feed each other (e.g., Reicher & Haslam, 2016). For example, violence of one group toward another (be it a "terrorist attack" or a "military operation") often leads to more support of violent actions of revenge by the other group, creating a cycle of intergroup aggression. As such, an analysis of the dynamics of intergroup violence is useful in understanding radicalization and terrorism. This interplay between different groups can also be witnessed in confrontations between groups with extreme right-wing ideas and extreme left-wing ideas. Moghaddam (2018) refers to this phenomenon of intergroup stimulation as "mutual radicalization." This process of mutual radicalization implies that it is useful to focus on a broader context including competing groups if one aims to understand the radicalization of one group.

Scope and outline of the book

In terms of the scope and aims of the book, we mainly focus on the psychological aspects of radicalization. However, we do include insights from various other disciplines, such as political science, pedagogics, and criminology, as we believe a multidisciplinary approach is most fruitful in understanding the process of radicalization.

This book consists of 10 chapters. After the current introduction, in Chapter 2, we define radicalization and discuss the difference between radicalism and notions such as fundamentalism and extremism. To illustrate this definition, we present a brief overview of different radical groups. Throughout the following chapters, our aim is to use studies about and examples of various radical groups. However, given the current focus on Islamic radicalization, this group will receive somewhat more attention throughout the book than other groups.

Chapter 3 deals with methodological questions. The use and merits of qualitative and quantitative methods are described, as well as the general question concerning the strengths and limitations in carrying out empirical and primary research in this area. Finally, relevant ethical considerations are discussed.

In Chapter 4, we discuss the process of radicalization. What does it mean to view radicalization as a process, and what are its general characteristics in terms of causality, (non-)linearity, speed, and so on? Furthermore, we specify between three phases of radicalization (i.e., from a vulnerability phase to a group phase to an action phase) in a way that leaves room for the various (root) causes and individual characteristics that are discussed in the following chapter.

In Chapter 5, we discuss personal characteristics (e.g., demographics such as gender and age). Is it possible to sketch a profile of a typical radical person?

In addition, we present a typology of radical(izing) individuals based on their basic motivations. This typology is an integration of previous work in this area. We present empirical studies (from the U.S. and The Netherlands) to illustrate this typology. At the same time, we articulate clearly that any typology has limitations. They can be used to provide an overall picture of radical people, but it is always difficult to stick a label to an individual. People can be more than one "type": people might change, and certain "types" may be more relevant in certain contexts than in others (i.e., they can be situation specific). In this chapter, we also discuss the relationship between radicalization and mental health: the object of a growing body of academic work. Here, the question is raised: to what degree can radical individuals and their basic motivations be considered "normal"?

In Chapter 6, we focus on the psychological determinants of radicalization at the group level. We describe determinants of radicalization at the meso (group) level. Subsequently, we describe processes that can occur when people have decided to join a radical group (such as social influence processes). In addition, we outline how radical groups prepare their members for violent actions.

In Chapter 7, we focus on the factors that can trigger people to become more (or less) radical. Specifically, a process of radicalization is often characterized by sudden changes due to trigger events in a person's life. This chapter describes these trigger events. In addition, we discuss findings from studies on trigger factors from various countries and radical groups.

In Chapter 8, we examine how people can be(come) resilient against extreme influences. Traditionally, people have conceptualized resilience in terms of coping reactions of individuals, groups, or nations following a disaster (such as a terrorist attack). However, we focus on a different type of resilience: how (potentially vulnerable) people can resist propaganda from extremist groups. We discuss programs to increase resilience in the U.S., Europe, and Australia.

In Chapter 9, we discuss the issue of deradicalization. What does deradicalization entail? When is someone deradicalized? We discuss the various forms of deradicalization (i.e., leaving behind the group and/or leaving behind the ideas). Subsequently, we describe the factors that contribute to (de)radicalization. Importantly, the factors driving deradicalization are not always the same as the reverse of the factors that stimulate a process of radicalization.

In Chapter 10, we first translate our analysis to practical implications and make recommendations for applied researchers. We also describe in more general terms the pitfalls of doing research in this area. Second, we outline practical implications and recommendations for policy makers and practitioners. For these recommendations, among other sources, we use the results of various expert meetings with local practitioners and municipalities.

Bibliography

Alonso, R. (2006). *The IRA and armed struggle.* London: Routledge.

Baeyer-Kaette, W., von D. Classens, H., Feger, H., & Neihardt, F. (Eds.). (1982). *Analysen zum terrorimsus 3: Gruppenprozesse.* Darmstadt: Verlag.

Berko, A. (2007). *The path to paradise: The inner world of suicide bombers and their dispatch-ers.* Washington, DC: Potomac Books.

Bloom, M. (2005). *Dying to kill: The allure of suicide terror.* New York: Columbia.

Buijs, F. J., Demant, F., & Hamdy, A. (2006). *Strijders van eigen bodem: Radicale en Democratische moslims in Nederland [Home-grown warriors: radical and democratic Muslims in the Netherland].* Amsterdam: Amsterdam University Press.

Brislin, R. W. (1970). Back-translation for cross-cultural research. *Journal of Cross-Cultural Psychology,* 1(3), 185–216.

Carley, K. (2004). Estimating Vulnerabilities in Large Covert Networks. *Proceedings of the 2004 International Symposium on Command and Control Research and Technology,* San Diego, CA, 2004.

Chen, H., Chiang, R. H., & Storey, V. C. (2012). Business intelligence and analytics: From big data to big impact. *MIS Quarterly,* 36(4).

Dalege, J., Borsboom, D., van Harreveld, F., van den Berg, H., Conner, M., & van der Maas, H. L. (2016). Toward a formalized account of attitudes: The Causal Attitude Network (CAN) model. *Psychological Review,* 123(1), 2.

DiGrande, L., Perrin, M. A., Thorpe, L. E., Thalji, L., Murphy, J., Wu D., … , & Brackbill R. M. (2008). Posttraumatic stress symptoms, PTSD, and risk factors among lower Manhattan residents 2–3 years after the September 11, 2001 terrorist attacks. *Journal of Traumatic Stress,* 21, 264–273.

Dolnik, A. (2011). Conducting field research on terrorism: A brief primer. *Perspectives on Terrorism,* 5(2), 3–35.

Doosje, B., Zebel, S., Scheermeier, M. & Mathyi, P. (2007). Attributions of responsibility for terrorist attacks: The role of group membership and identification. *International Journal of Conflict and Violence,* 1, 127–141.

Doosje, B., Zimmermann, A., Küpper, B., Zick, A. & Meertens, R. (2010). Terrorist threat and perceived Islamic support for terrorist attacks as predictors of personal and institutional out-group discrimination and support for anti-immigration policies – Evidence from 9 European countries. *International Review of Social Psychology,* 22, 203–233.

Doosje, B., van den Bos, K., Loseman, A., Feddes, A. R., & Mann, L. (2012). "My In-group is Superior!": Susceptibility for Radical Right-wing Attitudes and Behaviors in Dutch Youth. *Negotiation and Conflict Management Research,* 5(3), 253–268.

Doosje, B., Loseman, A., & Bos, K. (2013). Determinants of radicalization of Islamic youth in the Netherlands: Personal uncertainty, perceived injustice, and perceived group threat. *Journal of Social Issues,* 69(3), 586–604.

Faul, F., Erdfelder, E., Buchner, A., & Lang, A.-G. (2009). Statistical power analyses using G*Power 3.1: Tests for correlation and regression analyses. *Behavior Research Methods,* 41, 1149–1160.

Feddes, A. R., & Gallucci, M. (2015). A literature review on methodology used in evaluating effects of preventive and de-radicalisation interventions. *Journal for Deradicalization*, WINTER 2015/16 (5), 1–27.

Feddes, A. R., Mann, L., De Zwart, N., & Doosje, B. (2013). Duale identiteit in een multi-culturele samenleving: Een longitudinale kwalitatieve effectmeting van de weerbaarheidstraining DIAMANT. *Tijdschrift Voor Veiligheid*, 12(4), 27–44.

Feddes, A. R., Mann, L., Leiser, A., Gringard, H., Wagenaar, W., Köhler, D., & Doosje, B. (2015). What motivates individuals to join and leave extremist groups? An interview study with 13 former right-wing extremists. Manuscript submitted for publication.

Hamers, H. J. M., Husslage, B. G. M., & Lindelauf, R. H. A. (2011). *Centraliteitsanalyses van terroristische netwerken*. Netherlands: Tilburg University.

Horgan (2009). *Walking away from terrorism: Accounts of disengagement from radical and extremist movements*. London: Routledge.

Jager, H., Schmidtchen, G., & Sulllwold, L. (Eds.). (1981). *Analysen zum terrorimsmus 2: Lebenslaufanalysen*. Darmstadt: Verlag.

Jamieson, A. (1990). Identity and morality in the Italian Red Brigades. *Terrorism and Political Violence*, 2, 508–520.

Jürgensmeyer (2000). *Terror in the mind of God*. Los Angeles, CA: University of California Press.

Liebert, R. M., & Liebert, L. L. (1995). *Science and behavior: An introduction to methods of psychological research*. New York: Prentice Hall. ISBN-10: 0131427210.

Lum, C., Kennedy, L. W., & Sherley, A. (2006). Are counter-terrorism strategies effective? The results of the Campbell Systematic Review on counter-terrorism evaluation research. *Journal of Experimental Criminology*, 2, 489–516.

Moghaddam, F. M. (2018). Mutual radicalization: How groups and nations drive each other to extremes. *American Psychological Association*. doi:10.1037/0000089-000

Nilsson, M. (2017). Interviewing Jihadists: On the importance of drinking tea and other methodological considerations. *Studies in Conflict & Terrorism*, 41(6), 419–432.

Post, J. M., Sprinzak, E., & Denny, L. M. (2003). The terrorists in their own words: Interviews with thirty-five incarcerated Middle Eastern Terrorists. *Terrorism and Political Violence*, 15, 171–184.

Pyszczynski, T., Abdollahi, A., Solomon, S., Greenberg, J., Cohen, F., & Weise, D. (2006). Mortality salience, martyrdom, and military might: The great Satan versus the axis of evil. *Personality and Social Psychology Bulletin*, 32, 525–537.

Rapoport, D. C. (2004). The four waves of modem terrorism. In A. K. Cronin, & J. M. Ludes (Eds.), *Attacking terrorism: Elements of a grand strategy*, (pp. 46–73). Washington, DC: Georgetown University.

Reicher, S. D., & Haslam, S. A. (2016). Fueling terror: How extremists are made. *Scientific American*, 24, 34–29.

Ressler, S. (2006). Social network analysis as an approach to combat terrorism: Past, present, and future research. *Homeland Security Affairs*, 2(2).

Schuster, M. A., Stein, B. D., Jaycox, L., Collins, R. L., Marshall, G. N., Elliott, M. N., ... , & Berry, S. H. (2001). A national survey of stress reactions after the September 11, 2001, terrorist attacks. *New England Journal of Medicine*, 345, 1507-1512.

Scientific American (January 15, 2015). Anthropologist seeks the roots of terrorism. Retrieved from www.scientificamerican.com on October 19, 2017.

Schuurman, B. (2018). Research on Terrorism, 2007–2016: A review of data, methods, and authorship. *Terrorism and Political Violence*, 1–16. doi: 10.1080/09546553.2018.1439023

Sparrow, M. K. (1991). The application of network analysis to criminal intelligence: An assessment of the prospects. *Social Networks*, 13(3), 251–274.

Steinhoff, P. G. (1976). Portrait of a terrorist: An interview with Kozo Okamoto. *Asian Survey*, 16(9), 830–845.

Tausch, N., Becker, J. C., Spears, R., Christ, O., Saab, R., Singh, P., & Siddiqui, R. N. (2011). Explaining radical group behavior: Developing emotion and efficacy routes to normative and nonnormative collective action. *Journal of Personality and Social Psychology*, 101, 129.

Valk, I. V. D., & Wagenaar, W. (2010). *Monitor racisme & extremisme: in en uit extreemrechts* (p. 136). Amsterdam: Amsterdam University Press.

Vidino, L. (2011) The Buccinasco Pentiti: A unique case study of radicalization. *Terrorism and Political Violence*, 23(3), 398–418.

Webber, D., Babush, M., Schori-Eyal, N., Vazeou-Nieuwenhuis, A., Hettiarachchi, M., Bélanger, J. J., ... , & Gelfand, M. J. (2018). The road to extremism: Field and experimental evidence that significance loss-induced need for closure fosters radicalization. *Journal of Personality and Social Psychology*, 114(2), 270–285.

Zulaika, J. (1996). The anthropologist as terrorist. In: C. Nordstrom, & A. C. G. M. Robben (Eds.), *Fieldwork under fire: Contemporary studies of violence and culture* (pp. 206–223). Berkeley, CA: University of California Press.

Chapter 2

What is radicalization?

Goals

- Provide a definition of radicalization and terrorism.
- Present an overview of different radical groups.

Introduction

In Chapter 1, we indicated why we think it is important to study the process of radicalization from a psychological perspective. In addition, we described the process of radicalization in two examples (Mohammed Bouyeri in Box 1.1 and Anders Breivik in Box 1.2). In this chapter, we introduce the concept of radicalization and present a definition. Next,, we present an overview of different radical groups, and in the final section, we provide a summary of the main points.

Even though research on terrorism has had a long tradition, radicalization as a term became popular mostly after the 9/11/2001 attacks on the United States. At first, people (e.g., security services, politicians, and scientists) were interested in finding a profile of "the typical terrorist" (e.g., Horgan, 2006). This turned out to be difficult for several reasons. The most important one is that there are not many terrorists, and they tend to differ from each other, for example, in terms of their ideology. As these difficulties became more apparent, it has become clear that it might be more fruitful to focus on radicalization as a *process* that may lead to terrorism. This makes it possible to include more people in studies, as there are more radical people than there are terrorists (e.g., Moghaddam, 2005). At the same time, the concept of radicalization has led to some controversy. For example, some have argued that while terrorism can be relatively easily defined because it is a clear concept, a clear definition of radicalization may be more difficult to give because it is a fuzzier concept (Colaert, 2017; Coolsaet, 2011; Neumann & Kleinmann, 2013; Schmid, 2013).

Definition of radicalization

We define radicalization as a non-linear process in which people adopt an increasingly extreme set of ideas, often accompanied by an increased support for the use of violence by others and/or intention to use violent means themselves against perceived threatening out-groups in order to achieve political and/or societal changes (see Doosje et al,, 2016). Schmid (2013, p. 18) defines radicalization more elaborately as "an individual or collective (group) process whereby, usually in a situation of political polarisation, normal practices of dialogue, compromise and tolerance between political actors and groups with diverging interests are abandoned by one or both sides in a conflict dyad in favour of a growing commitment to engage in confrontational tactics of conflict-waging. These can include either (i) the use of (non-violent) pressure and coercion, (ii) various forms of political violence other than terrorism or (iii) acts of violent extremism in the form of terrorism and war crimes. The process is, on the side of rebel factions, generally accompanied by an ideological socialization away from mainstream or status quo-oriented positions towards more radical or extremist positions involving a dichotomous world view and the acceptance of an alternative focal point of political mobilization outside the dominant political order as the existing system is no longer recognized as appropriate or legitimate." Thus, radicalization is a process that may lead to both normative (often legal) and non-normative (often illegal) forms of protest and actions that may include the intention to use violence. It is non-linear, which means that it is not a simple and steady process but rather a process with bumps and sudden changes, often instigated by trigger events in a person's life (Feddes, Nickolson, & Doosje, 2016).

Importantly, this definition is different from terrorism, which has been defined as "an act of violence (domestic or international), usually committed against non-combatants, and aimed to achieve behavioral change and political objectives by creating fear in a larger population" (Doosje et al., 2016, p. 79). Similarly, Schmid (2011, p. 86) defines terrorism as "on the one hand a doctrine about the presumed effectiveness of a special form or tactic of fear-generating, coercive political violence and, on the other hand, a conspiratorial practice of calculated, demonstrative, direct violent action without legal or moral restraints, targeting mainly civilians and non-combatants, performed for its propagandistic and psychological effects on various audiences and conflict parties." Thus, while terrorism is the act of violence, radicalization is the route that may end up in violence.

However, it is important to note that radicalization does not always lead to an act of terrorism. Most terrorists have followed a process of radicalization, but not every person who is radicalizing will end up committing a terrorist attack. Whereas some scholars claim that the term "radicalization" may not be useful, others have argued that most researchers believe in a process of radicalization involving several steps or phases (e.g., Neumann & Kleinmann, 2013).

Finally, fundamentalism can be conceptualized as a drive to live according to the fundamentals. Altemeyer and Hunsberger (1992, p. 118) define religious fundamentalism as "The belief that there is one set of religious teachings that clearly contains the fundamental, basic, intrinsic, essential, inerrant truth about humanity and deity; that this essential truth is fundamentally opposed by the forces of evil which must be vigorously fought; that this truth must be followed today according to the fundamental, unchangeable practices of the past; and that those who believe and follow these fundamental teachings have a special relationship with the deity."

Violent actions or terrorist attacks may serve multiple goals. First, they are meant to persuade other people of the importance of the terrorist's concern. In other words, it might be a strategy to make one's voice heard. Second, with these violent actions, terrorists may aim to influence those people who work in a particular field, to try to make them reconsider the work that they are doing. For example, by killing doctors who perform abortions, they hope to stop other doctors from performing (or starting to perform) abortions. Third, sometimes terrorists aim to instigate a reaction among either a general public or a government. As such, oftentimes, "terrorism is meant to hurt, not to destroy" (Crenshaw, 2000, p. 406). Rather, "Victims or objects of terrorist attack represent a larger human audience whose reaction the terrorists seek" (Crenshaw, 1981, p. 379). Finally, violent actions often aim to persuade politicians to address this issue, if not now, maybe later. As such, political changes can be a prime goal of terrorists.

After having defined the most central concepts (radicalization, terrorism, and fundamentalism), a couple of considerations are in place. First, radicalization can be a *normal* process. In fact, in their educational approach to radicalization, Van San, Sieckelinck, and de Winter (2013) argue that it might be good to conceive of radicalization as a process in which, in their terminology, "ideals have gone adrift." An important assumption in their work is that youngsters should be allowed to hold and cherish (radical) ideals and that it is a parent's or a teacher's task to merely steer these ideals in the right (i.e., pro-social) direction. As such, being radical in beliefs is fully accepted and even welcomed from their perspective.

Second, (religious) fundamentalism can take various forms. For example, in terms of Islamic fundamentalism, people have investigated the role of Salafism (e.g., Roex, 2014; Wiktorowicz, 2006). In terms of Salafism, it is possible to distinguish at least three sub-groups: (1) the apolitical Salafi sub-group, who is not at all interested in politics; (2) the political Salafi sub-group, who is politically interested but is opposed to the use of any form of violence; and (3) the Jihadi Salafi sub-group, who is motivated to achieve changes via violence if deemed necessary. This implies that fundamentalism in itself is often harmless. It only becomes problematic (i.e., potentially disobeying the law) when it is accompanied by a belief that it is both legitimate and effective to use violence to establish political or societal changes, and people start to act on this belief.

Third, as briefly hinted at in Chapter 1, in line with the intergroup perspective on radicalization and terrorism, we realize that one people's terrorist can be another people's freedom fighter. Whether a person is perceived as a freedom fighter or terrorist depends on the perspective and angle from which to look at an intergroup conflict. Do the Israeli people suppress the Palestine people by occupying Palestine (i.e., the land they owned before 1948), and can violence from the Palestine side be interpreted as performed by "freedom fighters"? Or do we have to conceive of Palestine people displaying violence as "terrorists"? Similarly, are the attacks by Israeli on Palestine targets acts of terrorism or acts by freedom fighters? It all depends on your point of view (often fueled by group membership), and this is true for most intergroup conflicts. In most conflicts, there are two sides of a coin.

After providing the definitions as well as some discussion points related to these definitions, in the next section, we provide an overview of the most important types of radical groups that exist in current societies.

Different radical groups

In this section, we present a brief overview of different types of radical groups. We make a distinction between the following types of groups: (1) nationalistic/separatist, (2) extreme right-wing groups, (3) extreme left-wing groups, (4) single-issue groups, and (5) religiously motivated groups. In Box 2.1, we present the five types of groups and their main concerns, and we present some examples of each group. In separate boxes (Box 2.2 to Box 2.6), we present a further description of one example of each group to illustrate key elements of this type of group.

Box 2.1   Different radical groups, their main concerns and examples

Type of group	Main concern	Examples
1. Separatist	Territory for the own group	ETA, IRA, Palestine/Israel, PKK
2. Extreme Right-Wing	Threat to superiority of the "white race"	Ku Klux Klan, Stormfront
3. Extreme Left-Wing	A fair distribution of wealth	FARC, RAF
4. Single Issue	One particular topic	Army of God, Animal Liberation Front
5. Extreme Religiously Motivated	Spreading their religion	ISIS, Al Qaeda, Al-Shabaab

Nationalistic/separatist groups

Once people feel they belong to a (national) group, they value clear distinctions between their own group and other groups. This is particularly apparent when it comes to borders between countries. Groups appreciate the territory that they possess and do not want other groups to cross their border and claim their territory – indeed, this unwanted invasion of own territory can instigate a full-blown war between neighboring countries.

However, in some cases, people feel that they belong to a certain (national) group, but they do not possess an own independent country. Thus, they may live on a territory, but this territory is part of another country and thus politically not an independent nation. This situation can instigate a strong wish for independence. This wish can be so strong that some people are willing to use violence to achieve this goal, sometimes after non-violent options have proven unsuccessful. Thus, a central element of nationalist or separatist groups is that they want to claim a piece of land for their own group and are prepared to use violent means to achieve this goal.

Several groups have opted to use violence against civilians to achieve an independent country. ETA in Spain and France (see Box 2.2; Figures 2.1 and 2.2), the IRA in Northern Ireland, and currently the Palestine/Israel-context and the PKK in Turkey and Syria are all examples of groups aiming for a separate state, and they do not shy away from using violent means.

Box 2.2   Example of nationalistic/separatist group: Euskadi Ta Askatasuna in Spain and France

Figure 2.1 The ETA symbol. (From Wikimedia.org.)

Figure 2.2 ETA members. (By un usuario de Indymedia Barcelona, CC BY-SA 2.0). (From https://www.abc.es/espana/20130829/abci-guardia-civil-sortu-201308282016.html.)

ETA stands for Euskadi Ta Askatasuna, which means "Basque Homeland and Liberty." This group was formed in 1959 by leftist students who were not satisfied with the Basque Nationalist Party. The group is active in the Basque region, which is in the southwest of France and the north of Spain. Its goal was to create a separate Basque country, a goal it shared with the political party Batsuna. However, while Batsuna opted for the normative route to changes, ETA (also) included non-normative, violent routes to achieve an independent Basque homeland.

The group was most active between 1968 and 2010. During that time, the group was responsible for killing 820 people and injuring thousands. The ETA was most deadly in 1978–80 (68, 76, and 98 people were murdered).

After several proclaimed cease fires that did not last, the cease fire of September 5, 2010, is still honored. The ETA has agreed to a disarmament, which was effected on April 8, 2017. Thus, although technically the ETA still exists, it no longer plans to use violence to achieve political or societal changes.

Extreme right-wing groups

Extreme right-wing groups take pride in their White identity. In their view, non-White people are inferior and the Whites are facing serious threats from non-White minority groups in their countries. For example, they fear that their countries will be "destroyed" by an "invasion" of Muslims, and/or they might fear that Black people are receiving too many benefits and privileges from the government. According to their ideas, their concerns are not being addressed satisfactorily by the current political powers. This stimulates their notion that they have to take things into their own hands and deal with their issues themselves. In some cases, they may resort to violence against members of non-White minority groups.

In addition, extreme right-wing groups often seek out confrontations with extreme left-wing groups. For example, they may plan a counter-demonstration to disturb a demonstration by extreme left-wing groups. Examples of extreme right-wing groups include the Ku Klux Klan (KKK; mostly active in the United States – see Box 2.3 and Figure 2.3), Combat18 (letter 1 = Adolf, letter 8 = Hitler), and Stormfront.

Box 2.3 Example of an extreme right-wing group: Ku Klux Klan in the United States

(a)

(b)

Figure 2.3 (a) The KKK symbol (Wikipedia). (b) Traditional KKK outfit (from Wikipedia, by Underwood & Underwood – Public Domain). (From https://commons.wikimedia.org/wiki/File:Ku_Klux_Klan_members,_March_17,_1922.jpg.)

The KKK is a good example to illustrate that radicalization and terrorism have had a long history, even if in the past people have not used these terms to describe the actions of the KKK. The existence of the KKK is divided into three periods: the first period (1865–1871) mainly in the southern states; the second period (1915–1944) mainly in the south, west, and midwest and the third period (1946–present) in the whole United States. At its height (around 1925), estimates of number of members range between 3 and 6 million people (McVeigh, 1999). Currently, it has around 5,000 to 8,000 members.

These groups share their pride in being White and their dislike for African-Americans in particular. The KKK strives for "a pure and clean" White (American) society, without it getting "stained" by non-Whites. The KKK is associated with violence, including lynching, toward African-Americans, often their leaders, but also ordinary African-American civilians. During the civil rights movement in the 1960s, it was active against members of this movement. Members of the KKK consider themselves Christians. However, no Christian denomination wants to be officially associated with the KKK.

In 1987, a jury found the KKK member Henry Francis Hays guilty of lynching an African-American, Michael Donald, in 1981. Hays was executed in 1997. As his action ostensibly was instigated by leaders of the KKK, the KKK were ordered to pay US$7 million. However, the KKK did not have enough financial means to pay the US$7 million. Even after selling their national headquarters in Tuscaloosa for $52,000, the KKK was basically bankrupt. At the moment, the KKK is not one group but consists of around 100 small groups across the United States.

Extreme left-wing groups

Extreme left-wing groups have been active throughout history, but were particularly active in the 1970s in European and South American countries. Their main influences stem from communism (Marxism in particular) and socialist ideas. Their main concern is a fair distribution of wealth in society – a theme that resonated well with many people in the 1970s. Extreme left-wing groups often fought against conservative regimes around the world. Groups included Red Army Faction in West Germany, the Red Brigades in Italy, the "Action Directe" (AD) in France, the Communist Combatant Cells (CCC) in Belgium, the Red Army in Japan, the Tamil Tigers in Sri Lanka (also an example of a separatist group) – see Box 2.4; Figures 2.4 and 2.5, the Sandinistas in Nicaragua, and Revolutionary Armed Forces of Colombia (FARC) in Colombia (see De Graaf, 2011).

Box 2.4   Example of an extreme left-wing group: Revolutionary armed forces of Colombia

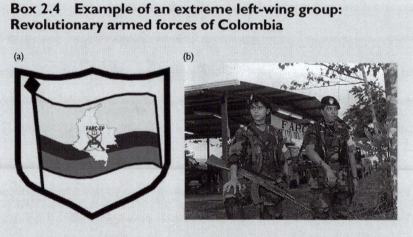

(a)   (b)

Figure 2.4 (a) The symbol of the FARC (Wikipedia). (b) FARC members (Wikipedia – DEA Public Affairs). (From https://www.flickr.com/photos/smoreno2007/2096338023.)

The FARC began in 1964 as a Marxist—Leninist movement of peasants advocating agrarianism and anti-imperialism. After the Colombian military attacked communist villages, the FARC was formed as the military wing of the Colombian Communist Party. In addition to standard military actions, the FARC made use of terrorist activities such as kidnapping and ransom. Still, even though the FARC was on the list of terrorist groups in most Western countries, in Latin America, this was not the case. Rather, they were seen as a legitimate military movement.

Around 2007, the number of members was estimated to be 18,000. Subsequently, the number of members declined, as did support from the Colombian public, who demonstrated against the FARC in 2008, when millions took to the streets (see Figure 2.5).

Figure 2.5 Anti-FARC posters in February 2008 (Wikipedia – Create Commons Attribution 2.0 Generic).

With support and numbers declining, the FARC decided to negotiate with the government around 2015 and signed a peace agreement in 2016. However, the first version of this agreement was not supported by a referendum, but the second version was. Consequently, on June 27, 2017, FARC handed over its weapons to the United Nations. After a couple of weeks, the FARC transformed into a legal political party (Common Alternative Revolutionary Force).

Single-issue groups

As the name indicates, these groups are defined by the fact that they have a single issue that they feel so strongly about that they are willing to put a great deal of energy into legal/non-violent and sometimes illegal/violent actions in an attempt to tackle this issue. Single issue groups are widespread. They include environmental groups, anti-globalization groups, anti-abortion groups (e.g., Army of God – see Box 2.5, Figures 2.6 and 2.7), anti-nuclear groups, and animal liberation groups.

Box 2.5   Example of a single issue group: Army of God (in the United States)

Figure 2.6 Army of God spokesman Donald Spitz holds Army of God banner. (From Donald Spitz, https://upload.wikimedia.org/wikipedia/en/7/7c/Donald_Spitz_holds_Army_of_God_Banner.jpg.)

Figure 2.7 Convicted abortion doctor murderer Paul Hill. Permission: PD-FLGOV. (From https://alchetron.com/Paul-Jennings-Hill.)

"Killing one person, saving thousands of lives. This is the sword of the Lord." That is the main argument put forward by the Army of God, an example of a single-issue group based in the United States. This is a loosely connected group of people who are convinced that performing an abortion is against God's wishes. They believe this, because in the Bible, it says that only God can determine when it is time for a person to pass away. This is not a task to be done by humans. At the same time, they are so much convinced that they want to save babies from being aborted that they have decided that for once they have to determine to take God's responsibility and kill a doctor who performs abortions. They justify their actions with quotes from the Bible, such as from Lamentations 2:19: "Arise, cry out in the night: in the beginning of the watches pour out thine heart like water before the face of the Lord: lift up thy hands toward him for the life of thy young children."

This group meets occasionally to discuss their arguments and plans. This group is still active in the United States.

Extreme religiously motivated groups

The final type of group is religiously motivated groups. As with most religious groups, their main concern is to make certain that their religion will be spread to other peoples and places. However, extreme religiously motivated groups consider their morals and ethics superior to all other non-believers. As they see other people as inferior and a threat to their own world and religious views, they see it as their holy duty to fight against these non-believers (e.g., Al-Qaeda in Box 2.6, Figures 2.8 and 2.9).

Box 2.6   Example of an extreme religiously-motivated group: Al-Qaeda (worldwide)

Figure 2.8 Flag used by Al-Qaeda.

Figure 2.9 Attacks in New York (September 11, 2001). (From https://commons. wikimedia.org/wiki/File:WTC_smoking_on_9-11.jpeg.)

Al-Qaeda is a Sunni Islamist terrorist group founded in 1988 by, among others, Osama bin Laden. This group originated from people who fought against the Soviet invasion of Afghanistan in the 1980s. Al-Qaeda follows a Jihadi-Salafist ideology, in which the superior past of the Muslim worldwide community is celebrated. They aim to re-establish this powerful position of Muslims in the world. This group perceives the West as a threat to this aim and thus as enemies, because in their view, the West is fighting wars against Muslims and is supporting foreign governments that suppress Muslims in their country (e.g., Israel; Guardian, 2001). Perceived humiliation plays an important role: "What America is tasting now, is something insignificant compared to what we have tasted for scores of years. Our nation (the Islamic world) has been tasting this humiliation and this degradation for more than 80 years. Its sons are killed, its blood is shed, its sanctuaries are attacked, and no one hears and no one heeds" (Bin Laden, 2001).

Al-Qaeda is responsible for attacks on numerous civilian and military targets. This includes the 1998 U.S. embassy bombings in Kenya and Tanzania (225 casualties, including 12 U.S. citizens); the 2002 Bali bombings (202 casualties); and, most deadly, the September 11, 2001, attacks in New York (2,606 casualties) and Washington (125 casualties and 265 casualties on the four planes). These latter attacks spurred a reaction by the U.S. government: it started the "War on Terror" (invading Afghanistan in October 2001 and Iraq in March 2003). Al-Qaeda mostly plans its attacks in Asia and in the Middle East. It is still active in Syria.

A great many conflicts and wars have been initiated on the basis of religious grounds throughout the history of humans. These conflicts between religious groups have been between countries (e.g., India and Pakistan) or within countries (e.g., Nigeria). Oftentimes, such groups have also used terror attacks as a means to fight for their cause.

Summary and discussion

In this chapter, we have defined radicalization and discussed the related concepts of terrorism and fundamentalism. Our main argument is that radicalization is a process in which a person becomes more extreme in ideas and actions, and this person is increasingly willing to support and or adopt violent means to achieve political or societal changes. Although radicalization does not automatically lead to terrorism, most terrorists went through a process of radicalization.

Subsequently, we have identified five different types of radical groups, namely (1) separatist groups, (2) extreme right-wing groups, (3) extreme left-wing groups, (4) single-issue groups, and 5) extreme religiously motivated groups. For each group, we have indicated their main concern, and we have given examples. In addition, for each type of group, we presented one group in more detail in five separate boxes. It is important to note that these types of groups do not cover all the radical groups that exist. In addition, one group can belong to more than one type. For example, the Army of God (Box 2.5) is presented as a single-issue group, because its main concern is abortion. However, it is equally possible to place the Army of God in the category of extreme religiously motivated groups. As such, we argue that our categorization is helpful in placing groups, but it is not a 100% waterproof system of classification.

References

Altemeyer, B., & Hunsberger, B. (1992). Authoritarianism, religious fundamentalism, quest, and prejudice. *The International Journal for the Psychology of Religion*, 2, 113–133.

Colaert, L. (2017). Introduction: "Radicalisation": Complex phenomenon, ambiguous concept. In: L. Colaert (Ed), *"De-radicalisation": Scientific insights for policy* (pp. 13–22). Brussels: Flemish Peace Institute.

Coolsaet, R. (Ed.) (2011). *Jihadi terrorism and the radicalisation challenge: European and American Experience* (2nd ed.). Farnham: Ashgate.

Crenshaw, M. (1981). The causes of terrorism. *Comparative Politics*, 13, 379–399.

Crenshaw, M. (2000). The psychology of terrorism: An agenda for the 21st century. *Political Psychology*, 21, 405–420.

De Graaf, B. (2011). *Evaluating Counterterrorism Performance*. London: Routledge.

Doosje, B., Moghaddam, F. M., Kruglanski, A. W., De Wolf, A., Mann, L., & Feddes, A. R. (2016). Radicalization and Terrorism. *Current Opinion in Psychology*, 11, 79–84. doi:10.1016/j.copsyc.2016.06.008

Feddes, A. R., Nickolson, L., & Doosje, B. (2016). Triggerfactoren in het radicaliseringsproces. *Justitiële Verkenningen (WODC)*, 22–48.

Horgan, J. (2006). *The psychology of terrorism*. London/New York: Routledge.

Moghaddam, F. M. (2005). The staircase to terrorism: A psychological exploration. *American Psychologist*, 60, 161–169.

Neumann, P., & Kleinmann, S. (2013). How rigorous is radicalization research? *Democracy and Security*, 9, 360–382. https://doi.org/10.1080/17419166.2013.802984

Roex, I. (2014). Should we be scared of all salafists in Europe? A Dutch Case Study. *Perspectives on Terrorism,* 8, 51–63.

Sageman, M. (2004). *Understanding terror networks*. Philadelphia: University of Pennsylvania Press.

Schmid, A. P. (Ed.) (2011). *The Routledge handbook of terrorism research*. London & New York: Routledge.

Schmid, A. P. (2013). *Radicalisation, De-Radicalisation, and Counter-Radicalisation*. The Hague: International Centre for Counter-Terrorism. Available at www.icct.nl/download/file/ICCT-Schmid-Radicalisation-De-Radicalisation-Counter-Radicalisation-March-2013.pdf, accessed January, 30, 2018.

Stephan, W. G., Ybarra, O., & Morrison, K. R. (2016). Intergroup threat theory.

Van San, M., Sieckelinck, S., & De Winter, M. (2013). Ideals adrift: An educational approach to radicalization. *Ethics and Education*, 8, 276–289.

Wiktorowicz, Q. (2006). Anatomy of the Salafi movement. *Studies in Conflict & Terrorism*, 29, 207–239.

Chapter 3

Describing the elephant when you are blind

Methods to study radicalization

Goals

- Provides an overview of the questions we should ask to determine strengths and limitations of methods to study radicalization.
- Reviews different methods that have been used to study radicalization as well as future directions.

Introduction

In August 1972, Patricia Steinhoff (1976) conducted a series of interviews with the terrorist Kozo Okamoto. Okamoto was one of three Japanese students who attacked Lod Airport (now Ben Gurion International Airport near Tel Aviv) on May 30, 1972. After taking their machine guns and hand grenades out of their suitcases on the conveyor belt, the attackers killed 26 individuals within two minutes. Nearly 80 other travelers were wounded. Against all odds, Okamoto survived the attack and was arrested. The other two attackers, who like Okamoto were from Japan and had attended universities, were killed.

How is it possible that Kozo Okamoto, a Japanese citizen, got involved in an attack in Israel that was sponsored by the Popular Front for the Liberation of Palestine, an Arab terrorist organization? What were his motives? What prepared Okamoto to shoot unarmed human beings? In short, what did his radicalization process until the moment of attack look like? Studying radicalization is a bit like the Indian tale about several blind men in a village who become aware of the arrival of a strange animal they do not know the shape or form of (see Figure 3.1). Each blind man focuses on a different part of the animal and, based on touch, describes this strange creature as slightly different than the other men do. For the study of radicalization, a similar tale can be told. Many different methods have been used and are being developed to study the subjects, who are often seen as strange creatures. Each method tells us a slightly different story about radicalization. A basic knowledge of the shortcomings and advantages of these different methods helps us to better understand and interpret the existing evidence.

Figure 3.1 Studying radicalization is a bit like the Indian tale about three blind men describing an elephant, a strange creature unknown to them: each focuses on a different part and takes his own view on what an elephant looks like.

In this chapter, we first discuss three questions that should be asked when considering the quality of methods to study radicalization: What do we want to measure (the research question)? How good is the measure (reliability and validity)? Can the measure predict future behavior (causality)? We then provide a brief overview of methods social scientists use to study radicalization and terrorism and address the strengths and limitations of each method. These include traditional methods such as experiments in the laboratory, surveys, interviews, and case studies. But we also discuss more recent developments in methodology such as network analysis and analyses of big data.

What it takes to have a good measure

A common assumption with regard to the quality of research on terrorism and radicalization is that it mostly consists of "thought articles" (literature reviews and theoretical discussions), and only little is based on "real" evidence (primary empirical data from interviews, surveys, or experimental work). For instance, Lum, Kennedy, and Sherley (2006) reported that only 3%–4% of 14 000 abstracts of articles published between 1971 and 2003 contained empirical data. A similar picture arose in a more recent review of 55 evaluations of the effectiveness of counter-radicalization interventions conducted between 1997 and 2014

(Feddes & Gallucci, 2015). While this may be the case, a review of the literature by Schuurman (2018) also provides a more optimistic picture of where the field is heading. Examining more than 3400 articles in leading journals on terrorism from 2007 to 2016, he points out a steady increase of empirical data and a wider variety of data-gathering techniques. This latter is a positive development because, as we will see, using a combination of different methods to study radicalization allows for compensating for the disadvantages each method unavoidably has.

In order to evaluate the quality of a study on radicalization, three questions should be asked: Is there a clear research question? How good is the measure? To what extent does the measure actually predict behavior?

The first question may seem simple at first, but think back to the three villagers describing the elephant. Randomly examining the strange creature is not the most effective manner. A good-quality study first makes explicit what the focus is; in other words, what is the *research question*? Do we focus on how the strange creature looks, or are we interested in how the strange creature behaves? In the context of studying radicalization, for example, the researcher can focus on aspects of the individual (e.g., "Are people who suffer from depression more attracted to violent groups or not?") or on aspects of the group (e.g., "How do social norms influence the willingness of group members to use violence?").

Once the research question has been specified, we need to determine the quality of the measure. In regard to the question of how good the measure is, two concepts are particularly important: reliability and validity. A measure is considered *reliable* if results can be replicated. This means that results that have been found in one study are found again if the study is repeated later in time or by other researchers. The more results are influenced by factors outside the control of the researcher (e.g., the weather, distractions to participants), the less reliable the measure. It follows, then, that results obtained in the controlled environment of a laboratory experiment (where the circumstances under which the study is conducted are kept constant) are considered more reliable than those of an experiment carried out in the real world, a so-called "field study." In a field study, irrelevant factors that are difficult to control may influence the results. For example, the presence of others when completing a survey may influence the answers a participant is willing to give.

Reliability also plays a role in other research methods such as conducting interviews or observation studies. Here, reliability scores can be calculated by taking the scores of two interviewers of observers and comparing the extent to which the results are similar (see, for example, Hallgren, 2012, for a demonstration of how to do this).

Another factor influencing reliability is *sample size*. The more participants in a study, the more reliable a study is or, in other words, the more *statistical power* a study has. Statistical power means the likelihood that a relationship or an effect between two variables (e.g., self-esteem and attitudes toward ideology-based violence) can be detected if it is truly there. A survey study with only 10 participants is considered low in reliability because it has low power. But is a survey study with 180 participants reliable? It may be, for example, that a survey study that includes a measure of self-esteem and a measure of attitudes toward violence does not find a significant relation between these two, while in reality, this association is there. To determine whether the number of participants in a study is sufficiently large to find an effect when it is, in fact, present, researchers conduct a "power analysis" (see Faul, Erdfelder, Buchner, & Lang, 2009, for a more detailed explanation of how to conduct a power analysis).

Validity is the second concept that is important in determining how good a measure is. Validity refers to the question of whether a method measures what it is meant to measure. A test may be highly reliable, as it is conducted in the controlled environment of a laboratory, but meanwhile very low in validity, as the results do not consider the complexity of the real world. This is called *external validity*. Laboratory experiments are often low in external validity, as they concern an artificial environment, and participants are aware they are being studied, which may influence their behavior or their answers on a task. Presumably, a field setting (e.g., in the participants' house or neighborhood) is an environment that an individual perceives as natural. The type of participants may also influence external validity. An often-heard criticism on laboratory studies on radicalization and terrorism is that these do not have radical individuals or terrorists as participants. In this respect, interview studies and surveys conducted with (former) terrorists have higher external validity.

The third question relates to the conclusions we can draw about whether a measure actually predicts behavior. More widely, *causality* refers to the question of whether one variable *predicts* another variable and not vice versa. For example, does an increase in self-esteem in individuals result in an increase in support for the use of ideology-based violence? Or is it that higher levels of self-esteem are a result of the fact that an individual is becoming more supportive of the use of ideology-based violence? Questions of causality can only be answered by using an *experimental* or *longitudinal* research design. In an experiment, the researcher systematically varies a variable. For example, Pyszczynski and colleagues asked individuals in an experimental condition to think about their own death in one condition (Pyszczynski et al., 2006). After that, the researchers measured support for the use of violence. They then compared the results to a control condition in which individuals did not have to think about their own death but only answered the questions to measure support for violence. This experimental design allows us to conclude whether a change in one variable (in this case thinking about death) results in more support for violence. In survey studies that are conducted at one point in time, no variable is systematically changed. All variables are measured

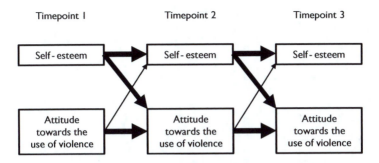

Figure 3.2 Fictitious example of a longitudinal study that investigates the relation between the variables self-esteem and attitudes toward the use of ideology-based violence. The variables are measured at three time points. Broader lines indicate stronger relationships.

at the same time (a so-called *correlational study*), which does not allow us to draw conclusions about whether one variable leads to another.

In a longitudinal study, however, the same measure is presented to participants at different points in time. Take, for example, the question of whether self-esteem is related to more positive attitudes toward violence. In a longitudinal study, a researcher presents a survey to participants at different points in time: at the beginning of the year (Timepoint 1), halfway the year (Timepoint 2), or the end of the year (Timepoint 3). Then the researcher calculates the results for self-esteem and attitude toward violence at each time point. In Figure 3.2, the (fictitious) results are given. The broader arrows indicate a stronger relationship between two variables. For example, individuals who have high self-esteem at Timepoint 1 are also likely to have high self-esteem at Timepoints 2 and 3. The arrows from self-esteem at Timepoints 1 and 2 that lead to, respectively, attitude toward violence at Timepoints 2 and 3, however, are broader than those going from attitude toward violence toward self-esteem. This would then be evidence supporting the causality hypothesis that higher self-esteem results in more positive attitudes toward the use of violence.

In sum, the lesson to be learned here is to critically consider each method used in a study and know well the advantages and disadvantages of each method in regard to the conclusions that can be drawn based on the results. As an illustration, in Table 3.1, several studies are presented that study different aspects of radicalization. Each study uses different methods in doing so. Notably, using different methods to study the same research question (a so-called *multi-method approach*) is recommended, as the different methods can complement each other. For example, Webber et al. (2018) used both experiments and field studies to examine the role of loss of significance in the radicalization process (see Box 3.1 for a description of their field studies).

Table 3.1 Examples of different studies on radicalization using different methods and some issues regarding reliability and validity

Example of study	Method used	Reliability considerations	Validity considerations	Causality consideration
Pyszczynski et al. (2006)	Experimental study	High because of controlled environment, which limits the influence of irrelevant factors.	External validity is low, as participants are students who were not radicals or (former) terrorists.	As this study incorporated an experimental design, it allows for causal statements about whether one variable affects another variable.
Doosje, Loseman, and Van den Bos (2013)	Survey study	High, as previously validated scales were used to measure constructs and it concerns a large number of participants.	The criticism on this study could be that external validity is low, as it concerns high school students who were not radicals or terrorists.	It concerns a measurement at one point in time. This method only allows us to say something about associations between different variables but not whether one variable leads to another.
Steinhoff (1976)	Interview study	Reliability can be considered low, as it concerns only one interview. If the interview excerpts were written out and evaluated by different researchers, then inter-rater reliability could be measured.	External validity is high, considering it concerns an interview with a former terrorist; the question can be asked whether this interview can be generalized to other terrorists.	The interview method provides a rich amount of information about different variables that may contribute to radicalization, but it does not allow conclusions/statements about causality.
Vidino (2011)	Case study	Again, reliability may be low, as it concerns a study of one specific case of radicalization and no standardized measures are used.	External validity can be considered high, as an actual case of Islamic radicalization is discussed.	As for the interview method, a case study does not allow us to say something about causality.
Webber et al. (2018)	Combination of experiments and survey studies	The experiments are considered reliable, as they are conducted in the controlled environment of the laboratory. The method is described in detail so the experiment can be replicated.	The field studies have high external validity, as they concern former terrorists. This complements the disadvantage of the experimental studies in which students participated who were not terrorists.	The experiments in this study allow us to say something about whether one variable leads to another. The survey studies do not, as they measure all variables at the same time.

Box 3.1   The road to extremism

Webber et al. (2018) used a field survey to examine whether and how significance loss (situations that make a person feel ashamed, humiliated, or demeaned) can result in greater anxiety in an individual, making him or her more susceptible to radicalization. In two survey studies, they found support for this hypothesis. The first study was conducted among 74 male imprisoned members of the Abu Sayyaf Group, a violent Islamic separatist group in the southern Philippines. The second study was conducted among 237 former members of the Liberation Tigers of Tamil Eelam (LTTE) in Sri Lanka who were in prison at the time of the study.

All instructions and materials were presented in the official language of the participants. For example, in the first study in the Philippines, this was the Tagalog language. Scales were translated from English to Tagalog and back-translated. Back-translation is a procedure that is used in cross-cultural research to make certain that the items capture the intended meaning in different languages (see, for example, Brislin, 1970). The researcher first writes a set of questions or passages in his or her (source) language following a set of rules (i.e., use simple sentences, use nouns rather than pronouns, avoid metaphors, avoid passive tense). A bilingual individual then translates from the source to the target language. A second bilingual then blindly translates back from the target to the source. If the two versions are identical, this suggests that the target version equals the source.

The survey data in the study by Webber et al. (2018) were analyzed using the statistical method of *regression analyses*. In both studies, it was found that the more the participants felt feelings of shame and humiliation in daily life (which are indicators of significance loss), the higher their need for closure (seeking a sense of certainty and meaning in life) and the greater their support for extremism (measured by items such as "Killing is justified when it is an act of revenge"). The result of the first study among Islamic militants from the Abu Sayyaf Group is shown in Figure 3.3. According to the

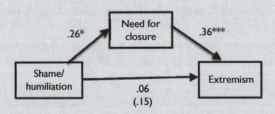

Figure 3.3 Results from regression analyses showing that higher levels of shame and humiliation are associated with a higher need for closure and, in turn, higher levels of extremism. (From Webber et al., 2018. Used by permission of the American Psychological Association.)

researchers, these results suggest that some responses to terrorism, such as banning Muslims from entering a country, can result in further marginalization of these people, increasing negative emotions such as shame and humiliation. This may actually lead to *more* extremist behavior.

An overview of methods that are commonly used

In this section, we discuss in greater depth several methods that social scientists use to study radicalization. As discussed in the previous section, each method has its advantages and disadvantages when considering issues of reliability, validity, and causality.

Case studies and interviews

Case studies and interviews provide us with a wealth of information about radicalization. They often focus on a single individual or several individuals (the "case"). Studies have been conducted with individuals in all three phases of radicalization depicted in our theoretical model on p. ix: "vulnerability phase" (e.g., Buijs, Demant, & Hamdy, 2006; Feddes, Mann, De Zwart, & Doosje, 2013), the "group phase" (e.g., Baeyer-Kaette, von D. Classens, Feger, & Neihardt, 1982; Horgan, 2009), and the "action phase" (e.g., Steinhoff, 1976; Jamieson, 1990; Post, Sprinzak, & Denny, 2003). Many interviews have been conducted with so-called "formers," individuals who were members of terrorist groups in the past and are willing to talk about their experiences.

Some researchers have joined terrorist groups to get an insider's view (Zulaika, 1996) or have gone to conflict areas to interview subjects, such as the anthropologist Atran (2010) and the Danish researcher Nilsson (2018), who interviewed both former and active Jihadi foreign fighters in Iraq and Lebanon. Several researchers have now stressed the importance of going out of the laboratory and into the field to get a better understanding of processes of radicalization (see also Ginges, Atran, Sachdeva, & Medin, 2011; Atran, Axelrod, Davis, & Fischhoff, 2017). This approach of collecting data in the field through various measures is called "participant observation" and is explained in more detail in Box 3.2.

Case studies and interviews are sometimes a first step in the research process, as they provide the basis for formulating research questions that can then be tested in larger populations using surveys and experiments. In the aftermath of the murder of filmmaker Theo van Gogh by Islamic extremist Mohammed Bouyeri in Amsterdam in 2004, Buijs et al. (2006) examined documents that described the family background of Bouyeri, his education, his membership in the extremist Hofstad group, and negative confrontations with authorities

Box 3.2   Participant observation

Participant observation is a field research method that is commonly used by anthropologists and sociologists. The researcher systematically describes behaviors and events in the natural setting of the person or group that is subject of the study. Participant observation involves the use of different methods such as informal interviews and taking detailed notes while participating in day-to-day life. Participant observation can increase the validity of a study by examining concepts directly in the field, thereby collecting real-world evidence (external validity). It is also a valuable method for generating research questions and hypotheses that can then be tested with other methods such as surveys and experiments. For instance, Atran (2010) used participant observation when studying Muslim fighters on the Indonesian island of Sulawesi to examine the importance of group identities in explaining an individual's willingness to die for a sacred cause.

he had. The procedure used by Buijs et al. is commonly used and provides a good example of a retrospective analysis of the trajectory of terrorists. Starting from the observation that, in particular, second-generation young Moroccan immigrants were represented in the radical Islamic extremist movement, Buijs and colleagues made a distinction between democratic and radical youngsters. In answering the question of what drove Dutch youth to become democratic or radical, Buijs et al. conducted in-depth interviews with 16 Moroccan-Dutch non-radical Muslims and 22 Moroccan-Dutch radical youths. The interviews were semistructured, which means that several questions were created beforehand, but interviewers were also allowed to explore further new topics that came up during the interview.

Thus, interviews and case studies are an excellent method for gaining insight into factors that play a role in processes of radicalization. They are a rich source of descriptive information (i.e., illustrating some form of behavior) and provide evidence to build, support, or (in)validate theories. Detailed accounts are given of phenomena that are often lost in narrow-focused experimental studies or in surveys.

One difficulty in conducting this research is finding participants. To get in touch with participants, Buijs et al. (2006) first conducted pilot talks with individuals from the neighborhood they focused on. These included people from (religious) neighborhood organizations (community houses, mosques), first-line workers, and educational settings and organizations (e.g., Islamic student organizations). By starting with these exploratory talks, the researchers were able to contact active democratic Muslim youngsters. Interviews typically lasted three to four-and-a-half hours, and some youngsters were interviewed multiple times.

Researchers studying radicalization sometimes actively share their methods of finding participants (e.g., Sikkens, Van San, Sieckelinck, Boeije, & De Winter, 2017). They also frequently make use of secondary sources such as families and friends of extremists and public records related to extremists such as police databases (Vidino, 2011; Weenink, 2015).

Experimental work

One of the most important tools of social scientists to predict behavior, including radical or terrorist behavior, is the experimental method. Psychologists have conducted experiments to test their predictions in the carefully controlled, but also artificial, context of a laboratory. One example is the above-mentioned work by Pyszczynski and colleagues (2006). Pyszczynski and colleagues tested the hypothesis that being confronted with one's mortality increases support for terrorist violence. Their research started from the observation that threats to a cultural worldview and self-esteem, experienced injustice, and humiliation are root causes underlying terrorism. Building further on this notion, the authors predicted that a threat to one's own existence (also called "mortality threat") can increase support for violent solutions. They tested this hypothesis among 40 Iranian students. Students were told beforehand that the experiment was about the effects of personality on impression formation to prevent students guessing about the goal of the study.

In the experimental condition, students were then asked to write down their thoughts about their own death and what will happen when they die. This request was presented as being a newly developed personality measure, while it actually was the mortality threat manipulation. In the control condition, students answered similar questions but about dental pain. In the second phase of the experiment, the students were presented with two fictitious questionnaires completed by two fellow students, one supporting martyrdom attacks and one opposing martyrdom attacks. Students were then asked a series of questions such as "How much do you think you would like this person?" and "Rate the degree to which you would consider joining their cause." The results of the study were in line with the predictions made by terror management theory: thoughts of death led Iranian participants to be more favorable toward martyrdom and more willing to join the cause. In a second study among 127 American students, the researchers found similar results in that students in the mortality threat condition responded more positively to statements such as "If we could capture or kill Osama bin Laden we should do it, even if thousands of civilians are injured or killed in the process." The researchers pointed out that reminders of death can have dramatic consequences for support of extreme violence to solve global conflicts.

While experimental work is useful in studying specific research questions related to causality, it is usually done in non-extremist populations, thereby lacking external validity. One solution to this shortcoming is using multiple methods in parallel, the *multi-method approach*. An example is the previously discussed work by Webber et al. (2018), who conducted two online experiments with American civilians on the role of significance loss-induced need for closure and how this fosters radicalization. The experimental studies complemented the two survey studies, making it a good example of how multiple methods are used in different populations (surveys among extremists and experimental studies among non-extremists) to test theoretical predictions. The experimental method allows for a careful analysis of certain processes in a controlled environment. As was discussed earlier, the great advantage of experiments is that researchers can draw conclusions about causality.

Surveys

Surveys have been widely used to study processes of radicalization. For example, Doosje, Van den Bos, Loseman, Feddes, and Mann (2012), Doosje et al. (2013), and Feddes, Mann, and Doosje (2015) used this method to study which variables are associated with more positive attitudes toward the use of ideology-based violence among non-radical individuals in the Netherlands. Tausch et al. (2011) used this method to study the question what variables predict support for extreme violence to create political change in Germany, India, and the UK. In a typical survey, constructs of interest are measured using a Likert-scale format. For example, to measure attitudes toward right-wing extremist ideology-based violence, Doosje et al. (2012) used four items, such as "I can understand right-wing extremists who use violence against others." Participants can then give an answer on a Likert scale, which ranges from 1 (= I totally disagree) to 5 (= I totally agree). The scores on the items are averaged, providing a mean score for each individual. The scores of each individual are then averaged to get the mean score of the whole group of participants.

The advantage of survey studies is that they often do not involve much time to complete and are easy to complete using online programs or paper-and-pencil formats. In Box 3.1 (presented earlier), an example is given of a survey study by Webber et al. (2018), who investigated associations between significance loss and extremism.

Survey studies have the advantage over interview studies and experiments that data of larger samples are more easily collected, but self-evidently, in most cases, it will not be possible to collect large samples of individuals who are members of extremist groups or who have been members in the past. They are, therefore, often low in external validity unless, of course, the focus of the study is on non-extremists.

Survey studies examining radicalization are also often correlational (one measure in time) and do not allow for drawing conclusions about causality.

Some upcoming methods to study radicalization

Network analysis

One of the latest techniques used to study radicalization is network analysis (e.g., Ressler, 2006). Network analysis may help, for example, in studying how intervening in extremist groups affects group performance (e.g., Sparrow, 1991), or (more abstractly) examining development of extreme attitudes (e.g., Dalege et al., 2016). A network is a group of individuals (called *nodes*) who are connected to each other by lines (called *edges*). As long as each person is connected to each other at least indirectly, information can flow from one person to another. Network analysis is valuable, as it not only focuses on one individual but also includes the social network surrounding an individual. This allows for answering questions such as who the most powerful individual in a terrorist group is and what would happen to a group if this person were arrested.

For instance, Hamers, Husslage, and Lindelauf (2011) applied network analysis to identify important individuals in terrorist networks and examined how groups functioned if particular members were removed. Using a network approach, the researchers examined social networks in the terrorist network of Jemaah Islamiyah, who were responsible for the Bali bombings, and the network involved in the Al Qaida 9/11 attack. Hamers and colleagues distinguished between four phases in a network analysis of terrorist groups: (1) *initiation*, in which specialists on a certain domain (e.g., a police officer, a military advisor) work together with experts in statistical methods to create a model; (2) *collect data and classify*, making explicit who the members in a network are and who is connected to whom; (3) *analysis*, defining the "rules" of the model such as the importance of certain qualities (e.g., ability to communicate, leadership skills, ability to make bombs); (4) *actions*: based on the results of the network analysis, decisions can be made such as whether to take an individual into custody or which individual should be monitored.

Network analysis not only focuses on understanding connections between individuals in groups. Network analysis can also be applied to better understand psychological factors that are involved in processes of radicalization. An example is the psychological factor "attitude toward ideology-based violence." A researcher can measure psychological factors that are expected to be related to attitude toward ideology-based violence such as self-esteem, uncertainty, experienced injustice, identification with an in-group, trust in authorities, and so on. Network analysis then allows for an examination how these psychological factors are connected to each other and, importantly, how a change in one factor may affect other factors. Network analysis can also be used to generate hypotheses. (see Dalege et al., 2016). These hypotheses can then be tested in controlled experiments or field studies.

Big data

Besides network analysis, another often-mentioned future candidate for radicalization research is the use of big data (Chen, Chiang, & Storey, 2012). Big data refers to datasets and analytical techniques that are so large and complex that they require advanced data storage and management. Technologies that are being used in big data are, for example, *data mining*. Immense amounts of data can be gathered from the internet by web mining techniques. The previously mentioned network analysis could be used to analyze online groups, social multimedia sites, and social networking sites (e.g., Carley, 2004; Ressler, 2006).

Valuable data sources about terrorist groups and terrorist attacks have also been created in the past years that are being updated and serve as a source of data. One example is the *Global Terrorism Database* by the National Consortium for the Study of Terrorism and Responses to Terrorism (START) at the University of Maryland (https://www.start.umd.edu). This database is publicly available and includes information about more than 170 000 terrorist attacks around the world from 1970 with annual updates. Databases such as these help organize the enormous amounts of information about radicalization.

Summary

In the beginning of this chapter, we used the tale of several blind men investigating a strange creature as a metaphor for the study of radicalization. While different methods are available to study this highly complex phenomenon, it is important to note that each method has its advantages and disadvantages. Each method differs in terms of reliability, validity, and to the extent it allows us to draw conclusions about causality. Using a combination of different methods (a multi-method approach) to study radicalization is, therefore, good practice. Case studies and interview studies provide detailed information that can form the basis of formulating hypotheses that can then be tested using controlled experimental setups and surveys including large numbers of participants. Nevertheless, these methods do not solve the main challenges in studying the complex phenomenon of radicalization: how to gain access to extremist populations and how to collect representative data that can be generalized to a larger population. The radicalization research field is a lively one, where innovative methods are continuously being developed and improved to broaden the researchers' toolbox.

Recommended reading

Atran, S., Axelrod, R., Davis, R., & Fischhoff, B. (2017). Challenges in researching terrorism from the field. *Science, 355*(6323), 352–354.

In this paper, Scott Atran and colleagues propose their view on how to improve theorizing, the development and testing of research questions by using field data from terrorists, supporters, and host populations.

References

Atran, S. (2010). *Talking to the enemy: Faith, brotherhood, and the (un)making of terrorists.* New York: HarperCollins.

Atran, S., Axelrod, R., Davis, R., & Fischhoff, B. (2017). Challenges in researching terrorism from the field. *Science,* 355(6323), 352–354.

Baeyer-Kaette, W., von D. Classens, H., Feger, H., & Neihardt, F. (Eds.). (1982). *Analysen zum terrorismus 3: Gruppenprozesse [Analyses of terrorism 3: Group processes].* Darmstadt: Verlag.

Buijs, F. J., Demant, F., & Hamdy, A. (2006). *Strijders van eigen bodem: Radicale en Democratische moslims in Nederland [Home-grown warriors: radical and democratic Muslims in the Netherland].* Amsterdam: Amsterdam University Press.

Brislin, R. W. (1970). Back-translation for cross-cultural research. *Journal of Cross-Cultural Psychology,* 1(3), 185–216.

Carley, K. (2004). Estimating Vulnerabilities in Large Covert Networks. *Proceedings of the 2004 International Symposium on Command and Control Research and Technology,* San Diego, CA, 2004.

Chen, H., Chiang, R. H., & Storey, V. C. (2012). Business intelligence and analytics: from big data to big impact. *MIS Quarterly,* 36(4).

Dalege, J., Borsboom, D., Van Harreveld, F., Van den Berg, H., Conner, M., & van der Maas, H. L. (2016). Toward a formalized account of attitudes: the causal attitude network (CAN) model. *Psychological Review,* 123(1), 2.

Doosje, B., Van den Bos, K., Loseman, A., Feddes, A. R., & Mann, L. (2012). "My In-group is Superior!": susceptibility for radical right-wing attitudes and behaviors in Dutch youth. *Negotiation and Conflict Management Research,* 5(3), 253–268.

Doosje, B., Loseman, A., & Van den Bos, K. (2013). Determinants of radicalization of Islamic youth in the Netherlands: personal uncertainty, perceived injustice, and perceived group threat. *Journal of Social Issues,* 69(3), 586–604.

Faul, F., Erdfelder, E., Buchner, A., & Lang, A.-G. (2009). Statistical power analyses using G*Power 3.1: tests for correlation and regression analyses. *Behavior Research Methods,* 41, 1149–1160.

Feddes, A. R., & Gallucci, M. (2015). A literature review on methodology used in evaluating effects of preventive and de-radicalization interventions. *Journal for Deradicalization,* 5, 1–27.

Feddes, A. R., Mann, L., De Zwart, N., & Doosje, B. (2013). Duale identiteit in een multi-culturele samenleving: Een longitudinale kwalitatieve effectmeting van de weerbaarheidstraining DIAMANT [Dual identity in a multicultural society: a longitudinal qualitative evaluation of resilience training DIAMANT]. *Tijdschrift Voor Veiligheid*, 12(4), 27–44.

Feddes, A. R., Mann, L., & Doosje, B. (2015). Increasing self-esteem and empathy to prevent violent radicalization: a longitudinal quantitative evaluation of a resilience training focused on adolescents with a dual identity. *Journal of Applied Social Psychology*, 45(7), 400–411.

Ginges, J., Atran, S., Sachdeva, S. & Medin, D. (2011). Psychology out of the laboratory: The challenge of violent extremism. *American Psychologist*, 66, 507–519.

Hallgren, K. A. (2012). Computing inter-rater reliability for observational data: an overview and tutorial. *Tutorials in Quantitative Methods for Psychology*, 8(1), 23.

Hamers, H. J. M., Husslage, B. G. M., & Lindelauf, R. H. A. (2011). *Centraliteitsanalyses van terroristische netwerken [Centrality analyses of terrorist networks]*. Tilburg: Tilburg University.

Horgan (2009). *Walking away from terrorism: Accounts of disengagement from radical and extremist movements*. London: Routledge.

Jamieson, A. (1990). Identity and morality in the Italian red brigades. *Terrorism and Political Violence*, 2, 508–520.

Lum, C., Kennedy, L. W., & Sherley, A. (2006). Are counter-terrorism strategies effective? The results of the Campbell systematic review on counter-terrorism evaluation research. *Journal of Experimental Criminology*, 2, 489–516.

Nilsson, M. (2018). Interviewing Jihadists: On the importance of drinking tea and other methodological considerations. *Studies in Conflict & Terrorism*, 41, 419–432.

Post, J. M., Sprinzak, E., & Denny, L. M. (2003). The terrorists in their own words: Interviews with thirty-five incarcerated Middle Eastern Terrorists. *Terrorism and Political Violence*, 15, 171–184.

Pyszczynski, T., Abdollahi, A., Solomon, S., Greenberg, J., Cohen, F., & Weise, D. (2006). Mortality salience, martyrdom, and military might: The great Satan versus the axis of evil. *Personality and Social Psychology Bulletin*, 32, 525–537.

Ressler, S. (2006). Social network analysis as an approach to combat terrorism: Past, present, and future research. *Homeland Security Affairs*, 2(2).

Schuurman, B. (2018). Research on terrorism, 2007–2016: a review of data, methods, and authorship. *Terrorism and Political Violence*, doi: 10.1080/09546553.2018.1439023.

Sikkens, E., Van San, M., Sieckelinck, S., Boeije, H., & De Winter, M. (2017). Participant recruitment through social media: lessons learned from a qualitative radicalization study using Facebook. *Field Methods*, 29(2), 130–139.

Sparrow, M. K. (1991). The application of network analysis to criminal intelligence: an assessment of the prospects. *Social Networks*, 13(3), 251–274.

Steinhoff, P. G. (1976). Portrait of a terrorist: an interview with Kozo Okamoto. *Asian Survey*, 16(9), 830–845.

Tausch, N., Becker, J. C., Spears, R., Christ, O., Saab, R., Singh, P., & Siddiqui, R. N. (2011). Explaining radical group behavior: developing emotion and efficacy routes to normative and nonnormative collective action. *Journal of Personality and Social Psychology*, 101, 129.

Vidino, L. (2011). The Buccinasco Pentiti: a unique case study of radicalization. *Terrorism and Political Violence*, 23(3), 398–418.

Webber, D., Babush, M., Schori-Eyal, N., Vazeou-Nieuwenhuis, A., Hettiarachchi, M., Bélanger, J. J., … & Gelfand, M. J. (2018). The road to extremism: field and experimental evidence that significance loss-induced need for closure fosters radicalization. *Journal of Personality and Social Psychology*, 114(2), 270–285.

Weenink, A. W. (2015). Behavioral problems and disorders among radicals in police files. *Perspectives on Terrorism*. 9, 17–33.

Zulaika, J. (1996). The anthropologist as terrorist. In: C. Nordstrom, & A. C. G. M. Robben (Eds.), *Fieldwork under fire: contemporary studies of violence and culture* (pp. 206–223). Berkeley, CA: University of California Press.

Chapter 4

The stages of radicalization

Goals

- Show that radicalization is a process that extends over time and consists of a sequence of factors that can be divided into various stages.
- Show what kind of phase models have been developed and what we can learn from their strengths and weaknesses.
- Present our own distinction between phases of radicalization, which serves as the structure for the remainder of the book.

To unwitting bystanders, radicalization sometimes appears to take place overnight: a person that once was thought of as a tolerant and law-abiding citizen suddenly seems bent on violently overthrowing the system and willing to sacrifice others' wellbeing – or even their lives – for a higher cause. After such shocking realizations, we might feel the urge to look for the "seed" of that person's radicalization: something that was always there but that we have somehow overlooked. Or we might feel that there must have been an external event or circumstance that has left such a familiar person completely unrecognizable.

If there is one thing that scientific research on radicalization and terrorism has shown, however, it is that such clear-cut and unambiguous explanations are not to be found. As the following chapter will also make clear, the terrorist profile does not exist, or at the very least has not been identified yet (Horgan, 2008, 2017; Borum, 2011a; King & Taylor, 2011). There is also a broad consensus among scholars that radicalization is typically not a matter of instant transformation, caused by one single factor (Neumann, 2013). The chances of suddenly and inadvertently finding oneself to be radicalized are practically the same as the chances of magically waking up as the giant beetle that protagonizes Kafka's

The Metamorphosis. Instead, a closer look at the radical's biography typically points to a multitude of signs, processes, and crucial events that led him or her down this fateful path.

And it is this notion of a *path* that is crucial, given that these various factors that pull and push usually take place in a *sequence*, one after the other. Many models of radicalization therefore divide this process into various stages. And this is where it gets tricky. One the one hand, the advantage of these models – or any other model, for that matter – is that they offer clarity. They reduce the complexity of real life by offering a distilled or stripped-down version of it. But this also carries the risk of oversimplification and of overlooking individual cases of radicalization that might not fit the model's tight mold.

The current chapter explores this dilemma between the importance of a recognizable theoretical *process* on the one hand and the inclusion of the plethora of real-life *pathways* on the other. It discusses earlier theories that envisioned a process of clearly distinguishable, highly specified, and successive phases of radicalization, as well as later contributions that are skeptical of any possibility of distinguishing between such distinct stages in an all-encompassing model. We argue that the earlier models present an overly narrow, rigid, and deterministic view of radicalization, while other more complex models lose sight of the sequenced, phased nature of this process. We then try to find a middle ground by outlining or own view, in which we distinguish between the vulnerability phase, the group phase, and the action phase of the radicalization process. As we argue, radicalization generally does occur in a sequence, and identifying and explaining these steps is not only crucial to prevent radicalization but also to distinguish non-violent radicals from actual terrorists.

Of staircases, straitjackets, and conveyor belts – criticism of earlier phase models

Ever since radicalization became a topical issue in Western societies – mostly after the attacks of 9/11 – attempts have been made to model this process. In each of these models, radicalization is seen as a process that plays out over a certain period of time and involves different factors and dynamics. But that's as far as the similarities go. The majority of the models distinguish between successive phases, although not all of them do. Moreover, as we will see, these models differ in length and complexity and in the specific factors or dimensions of radicalization they include or emphasize. Theoretical convergence or consensus has been hampered by the fact that most of the attempts at modeling radicalization are isolated and make no reference to each other (King & Taylor, 2011, p. 603). Moreover, they are largely presented via metaphors without sufficiently detailing the process itself, which might also be part of the explanation why these models are rarely subject to rigorous data-driven testing (Horgan, 2017, 200).

Ironically, one of the few models that has in fact been tested is also one of the most "metaphorical," namely Moghaddam's Staircase to Terrorism (2005). In this early and influential model, Moghaddam envisions Islamic radicalization as a narrowing staircase toward terrorism. The staircase connects six floors in which distinct processes push an increasingly small portion of those starting on the ground floor in the direction of the top floor in which a terrorist act is committed (see Figure 4.1). On the ground floor, a relatively large group of people perceives its (material) conditions as unjust, especially compared to the situation of others. The individual subsequently explores its options to improve its situation on the first floor, and if it finds it does not have any influence, it directs anger and frustration to an external enemy – which happens at the second floor. The person in question might encounter like-minded individuals in terrorist groups and decide to join them, which brings it to the third floor. On this floor, strict mental divides between "us" and "them," between in- and outgroup, are imposed through the group, and group members disengage from psychological mechanisms that inhibit someone from harming themselves and others. The indoctrination is intensified on the fourth floor, where the individual also gradually takes on a specific role in the group through training. In the final and fifth floor, the individual is trained to kill (Figure 4.1).

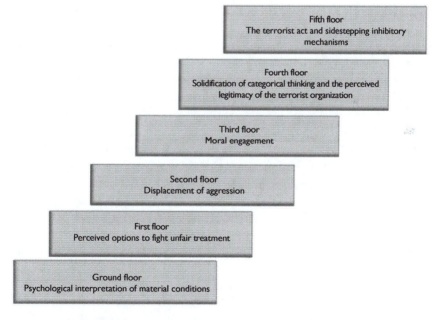

Figure 4.1 Moghaddam's Staircase to Terrorism. (From Borum, O. (2011b). *Journal of Strategic Security*, 4(4), 37–62.)

What most characterizes Moghaddam's (2005) model – the metaphor of the staircase – is also what it is most often criticized for. To start, the image of the staircase suggests a certain progressive linearity. In order to arrive at the final stage of committing a terrorist act, each floor must be traversed in a fixed order, which rules out the possibility of bypassing any steps. However, while most of the separate processes are supported by empirical evidence, there is no evidence for the *sequence* of these psychological mechanisms (Lygre, Eid, Larsson, & Ranstorp, 2011). Certain steps of the staircase might very well not be applicable in each and every radicalization process, and there is also a lack of empirical evidence for the transitions *between* the different steps or, in other words, for what precisely causes someone to move from one step to the other. Of course, the relatively large number of very specifically described stages in Moghaddam's staircase only worsens these problems, but the strength and urgency of this criticism also varies from one step to the next. The lack of causal explanation is especially problematic when it comes to the large step from radical thought to radical action, which in Moghaddam's model takes place between floors three and four (McCauley & Moskalenko, 2017, p. 4). We will come back to this distinction of ideas and action later. Other criticism of Moghaddam's model concerns its narrow view of radicalization in general. First of all, the model implies that radicalization is a rational problem-solving strategy used by an individual who faces an increasingly limited set of alternatives for action (Lygre et al., 2011, p. 609). This does not do justice, however, to the role played by emotions that many other scholars find in their research – see, for example, McCauley and Moskalenko (2011), Sageman (2008), and Della Porta (2013) – which may often not be so rational. Paraphrasing criminologist Yock Young, what needs to be captured is the adrenaline; the pleasure and the panic; the excitement; and the anger, rage, humiliation, and desperation (quoted in Rice, 2009, p.253). Second, and relatedly, Moghaddam's model exclusively focuses on aspects related to injustice and collective struggle, while the process of radicalization – as we will see in the next chapter – could just as well be propelled and driven by other personal "needs"; for example, the need for meaning, adventure, or identity. Finally, Moghaddam himself mentions that he aimed to describe only terrorist acts perpetrated by Islamic organizations, which already suggests a more limited perspective on possible shapes and trajectories of radicalization in general. Moghaddam's Staircase to Terrorism, then, is a good example of a model that does possess a certain clarity, distinctiveness, and empirical grounding but is ultimately too exclusive with regard to the variety of (other) pathways of radicalization: the phase model as a straitjacket.

Most other earlier models of radicalization largely face the same kinds of problems, and a brief review is useful to illustrate the various ways in which phase models can be overly exclusive and rigid. A good example of such an exclusive and rigid model was developed by Quinton Wictorowicz in his book *Radical*

Islam Rising: Muslim Extremism in the West (2005). Other influential models were funded or developed by government and/or law enforcement or security agencies: the New York Police Department (NYPD) model of Jihadization developed by Mitchell Silber and Arvin Bhatt (2007) and Tomas Precht's model of a "typical" radicalization pattern (Precht, 2007).

Where the large number of precisely defined phases made Moghaddam's staircase model especially vulnerable to criticism, these other models all make do with less. In fact, they all distinguish between four phases (Figures 4.2–4.4). They all start with a phase in which the individual is (or becomes) vulnerable and susceptible to radical ideas, and all feature a phase in which the individual joins a group and eventually legitimizes (or even perpetrates) violent terrorist acts.

These models are simpler and more straightforward than the Staircase to Terrorism, but they are similar to this model in their rigidity and the narrowness of their view on radicalization. For example, Wiktorowicz (2005), like Moghaddam, frames radicalization as solely springing from feelings of injustice, thereby overlooking any other motivating need. Moreover, practically all three models reserve a very important place for religion and (religious) ideology and conceptualize radicalization as a process of evolving beliefs and idea(l)s. Adopting or identifying with radical ideals – what Wiktorowicz calls "frame alignment" and what is called "self-identification" and "conversion and identification with radical Islam" in the NYPD's and Precht's models, respectively – becomes a precondition for joining the group, and indoctrination of these idea(l)s in later stages is often even implied to be sufficient for a turn to violence.

Figure 4.2 Wictorowicz's model of radicalization (2005).

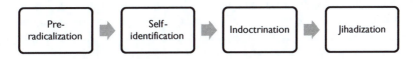

Figure 4.3 NYPD model of Jihadization (Silber & Bhatt, 2007).

Figure 4.4 Precht's model of a "typical" radicalization pattern (Precht, 2007).

Such explanations seem far from adequate. When it comes to joining a radical group, for example, other factors such as social affection, friendship, and love often are an equally important "lure" for the seeking individual (Veldhuis & Staun, 2009). Moreover, ideological "frame alignment" often takes place *after* joining, which is problematic since these linear progressive models imply that all the steps are necessary and in a fixed order.

Even more problematic is the explanation of the step toward violence. Such violence cannot be seen merely as an extension of the adoption of radical beliefs (e.g., Borum, 2011b; Crone, 2016; McCauley & Moskalenko, 2017). As is often remarked, not all radicals become terrorists. Even those who see violent acts as necessary do not always commit to such behavior themselves. The reverse is also not true, as not all terrorists are radicals in the sense that they uphold radical beliefs. Ideological beliefs might not always be the motivation behind violent acts; money, status, or thrill might simply exert a stronger pull. Explaining terrorist acts by *only* referring to ideology and religious beliefs therefore cannot be anything but a mischaracterization. And it has further consequences; it easily results in the problematic view that certain religious views unavoidably lead to terrorism and that radical (or even fundamentalist or orthodox) religious organizations are practically conveyor belts for terrorists[1]. It leads to a war of ideas, in which a much larger group is targeted than can reasonably expected to radicalize, which, ironically, might very well lead to feelings of discrimination and grievances that could in fact lead to radicalization and violence: a textbook case of self-fulfilling prophecy. According to some, the metaphor of the conveyor belt can be extended to phase models in general (Staun & Veldhuis 2009). Whether or not they focus on religion, these models generally take general traits as a cue that one is in a specific phase of the radicalization process, which only leads one way; reasons for leaving or reversing this path are often not included.

What the criticism amounts to, then, is that phase models are too much like straitjackets and conveyor belts. Straitjackets, because they focus too much on certain dimensions such as religion, the need for justice, ideology; because they view radicalization either as developing from the ground up, involving a "bunch of guys" that slowly evolve toward a radical mindset, or from the top down, where radicals are victims of the brainwashing done by radical leaders or preachers (Borum, 2011b); or because these models emphasize either situational factors or personality characteristics and not both (King & Taylor, 2011). Furthermore, they are reminiscent of conveyor belts to the extent that their rigid phasing and simple causal explanations evoke the image of a mechanical, automated process that unavoidably turns raw materials of "pre-radicalized" individuals into the "finished product" of a terrorist at the end of the belt. Instead, radicalization is a complex phenomenon, a combination of several dimensions, factors, and processes. In these models' defense, however, we have to recognize that they at least possess a certain clarity and distinctiveness and at least recognize that radicalization is a sequenced and (to some degree) ordered process.

Radicalization as a puzzle: Complex (phase?) models

While "simple" phase models exclude or overlook radicalization trajectories because of their overly narrow and rigid view of the process of radicalization, complex models aim to do justice to the multitude of trajectories by envisioning this process in a much looser and broader way. In fact, some authors even suggest letting go of the idea of a "phased" process altogether. As Hafez and Mullins argue, for example, the reality of radicalization is far too complex to describe as "an orderly sequence of steps or procedures that produce an output" (Hafez & Mullins, 2015, p. 959). They therefore propose to replace the notion of process with the idea of a puzzle, of which the pieces – being the factors that contribute to radicalization – can be put together in different ways, revealing diverse images depending on the context and the individual in question.

But this could easily lead to throwing out the babies with the bathwater. However diverse trajectories of radicalization might be, they always feature a certain sequence of events leading to radicalization and terrorism. In fact, even the puzzle metaphor points in the same direction, as any experienced puzzler would confirm. A certain sequence or temporal ordering is indispensable when putting those jigsaw pieces together, whether it is by first assembling the border, working your way out from one corner, or by starting with certain recognizable parts of the puzzle.

Some recent models of radicalization aim to retain a view of radicalization as a, at least to some degree, sequenced or "phased" process, while simultaneously aiming to do justice to the variety of factors and trajectories that might be involved. Subsequently, we will describe two models by McCauley and Moskalenko and (more briefly) by John Horgan in order to illustrate how these strike the balance between the need for a distinctive "process" on the one hand and the recognition of different "trajectories" for different people on the other. At the same time, as we will see, something valuable about the "outdated" simpler models might very well get lost in the complexity.

Pyramid model(s) of radicalization

Embracing yet another metaphor, McCauley and Moskalenko (2008, 2011) envision the radicalization process as a pyramid. This metaphor has some similarities to that of Moghaddam's (2005) dwindling staircase and, correspondingly, McCauley and Moskalenko also emphasize the relation between the terrorists that form the pyramid's apex and the base that is composed of a larger group of people that (potentially) sympathize with the terrorist's goals, or at least identify with a collective struggle. The layers or levels of the pyramid, however, are not primarily seen as floors or steps, but rather are composed of various mechanisms, with individual mechanisms (such as personal victimization or political grievances) featuring on the lower levels of the pyramid and group mechanisms (such as extreme cohesion under isolation and threat) and what they term mass mechanisms (such as dehumanization and martyrdom) forming the higher levels (see Figure 4.5).

Now there is a lot that can be said about the specific factors themselves and whether some factors are overlooked, but the authors themselves also state that the list is not definite (2008, p. 429). According to them, the most important thing is the idea that different combinations of factors, and not necessarily all of them, can come together – as jigsaw pieces – as a sufficient cause of radicalization. In the same vein, they emphasize that their model is not a staircase or a stage model, in the sense that all factors have to necessarily be applicable, in the same order, to result in violent extremist acts (2017, p. 13) – one can also "skip" levels when going up and down the pyramid.

At the same time, McCauley and Moskalenko also present another theoretical innovation that builds on the original pyramid model presented in 2008, namely the distinction between a pyramid of *action* and a pyramid of *opinion*. With this

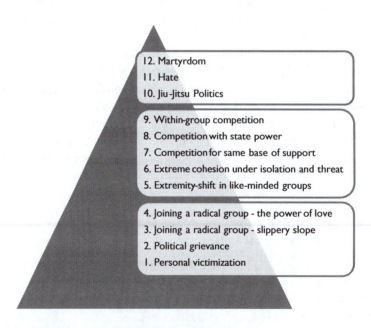

12. Martyrdom
11. Hate
10. Jiu-Jitsu Politics

9. Within-group competition
8. Competition with state power
7. Competition for same base of support
6. Extreme cohesion under isolation and threat
5. Extremity-shift in like-minded groups

4. Joining a radical group - the power of love
3. Joining a radical group - slippery slope
2. Political grievance
1. Personal victimization

Figure 4.5 McCauley and Moskalenko's pyramid model.

distinction, they aim to do justice to the earlier discussed criticism that, in their own words, "ninety-nine percent of those with radical ideas never act," while "many join in radical action without radical ideas" (2017, p. 21). The earlier described mechanisms, they argue, can often play a role in both pyramids and make the difference between being neutral or feeling morally obliged to use violence (being opposite ends of the opinion continuum), or being inert, an activist, a radical, or a terrorist (on the "action" continuum).

While the pyramid model(s) are unquestionably more nuanced and more adequately capture the complexity of radicalization, they also come at a loss. Analytically separating action and belief might lead to important insights, but it also poses the risk of overlooking how both dimensions interact. Even if beliefs by themselves are not good predictors of violence, they still might play a significant role in the path toward it (Neumann, 2013). And, contrary to what the authors suggest, a model that combines both "beliefs" and "actions" is not necessarily a conveyor belt that sees beliefs – or non-violent radical groups – as a steppingstone toward extremist violence. What such models do need to do, however, is make clear that the (last) step toward the stage of committing violence is not easily taken and involves a very specific combination of factors – not only the adoption of certain beliefs.

The pyramid model also dismisses radicalization's sequenced order too easily. It is telling that McCauley and Moskalenko, even though they insist that their model is not a stage model, do in fact often suggest or imply that radicalization consists of certain successive phases. As a response to their question "How do individuals move from the base to the extremes of terrorist violence at the apex?" (2008, p. 417), they often emphasize that an individual's radicalization is typically a "slow," "incremental," and "gradual" process, in which a person passes through various phases such as the gradual socialization within (small) radical or terrorist groups.

Of course, it is understandable that McCauley and Moskalenko do not simply label their 12 factors as successive steps, since that would amount to a process that is perhaps even more rigid than Moghaddam's staircase. The *types* of factors (individual, group, and society) are broader and more flexible and therefore perhaps better suited to represent a certain succession of stages of radicalization. Indeed, the individual factors do seem to point to earlier stages of radicalization (grievances, victimization, joining a group), while the group factors suggest a more advanced stage featuring further indoctrination and in- and out-group conflicts. It seems to be possible to conceive these stages in a broader fashion that captures the complexity and variety of radicalization processes but also retains their temporality and sequenced, gradual nature. The theoretical work of John Horgan, as we will see now, can be seen as an attempt to strike just this balance.

Reconciling complexity and temporality

In an article with Max Taylor, Horgan attempts to model the process of involvement in terrorism by acknowledging the complexity of factors involved, while also imposing some kind of temporal or sequenced order (2006). In that article, a distinction is made between setting events, personal factors, and the social/political/organizational context (see Figure 4.6). Without going too much into specifics, the sequenced nature of events is indicated not only by arrows, but also by accompanying descriptions of the types of factors. Setting events, for example, "relate to essentially past contextual influence" (2006, p. 592) and can therefore be said to pertain to an early stage of radicalization, a stage some 'simple' phase models would perhaps call "pre-radicalization." Indeed, Taylor and Horgan explicitly speculate about such temporal ordering of factors when they suggest that "features of setting events and personal factors seem likely to be most influential" in the "initial stage of involvement," after which, they hypothesize, "the relative weight of influence between "personal" and "social-political-organizational" changes," and the significance of the latter ultimately becomes decisive in "the later development of terrorism" (2006, p. 594) (Figure 4.6).

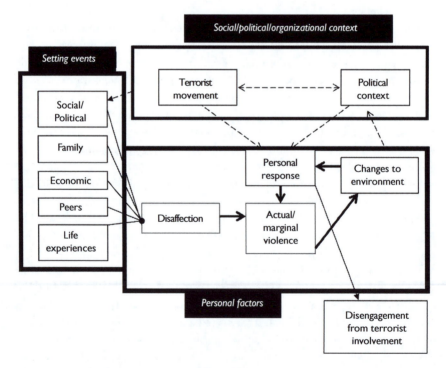

Figure 4.6 Taylor and Horgan's process of involvement with terrorism. (From Taylor, M. & Horgan, J. G. (2006). *Terrorism and Political Violence*, 18(4), 585–601.)

While Taylor and Horgan do not clearly define the separate stages of radicalization, Horgan himself does make such an explicit distinction in other work, where he states that the process of involvement in terrorism "comprises at least three seemingly distinct phases": becoming involved, being involved, and disengagement (2008). Such a distinction between phases does indeed square better with both the intuition and the empirical evidence that point, again, to the gradual and incremental nature of the radicalization process. At the same time – and this is perhaps why Horgan added the "at least" – the stages of radicalizations are very broad. Leaving out the disengagement phase, the process is essentially divided into the endpoint and the journey to it, which does not grant us that much more insight in the general order of factors. In the next paragraph, therefore, we take up the glove and attempt to sketch the outlines of a stage model that is further elaborated, a model, moreover, that will serve as the "stage" (no pun intended) for the elaboration of the specific factors in the subsequent chapters of this book.

Simple yet complex: Toward a new phase model of radicalization

Contrary to what the critics of phase models say, we argue that it is possible to distinguish between general successive stages of radicalization. These critics did make very valid points, however, and therefore a phase model of radicalization needs to fulfill certain requirements. First, it should not be too narrow in its view of radicalization. It should not focus only on one personality trait or psychological need, recognize one specific dimension of radicalization – such as a religious, cognitive, or political dimension – or only emphasize either pull or push factors. Second and relatedly, a phase model of radicalization should give ample attention to the causal mechanisms behind transitions between phases. In other words, why do people move from one phase to the next? Given the previous, this explanation will never consist of only one factor but should always include a variety of reasons. And in the case of the step toward violent acts, this explanation needs to be especially convincing, as there are many more radicals than terrorists. Finally, a phase model of radicalization should also elaborate upon why and when people do *not* radicalize further: when they go back (deradicalization) or take a different path. In other words, it should include protective factors against radicalization or factors that result in deradicalization or disengagement. Again, a phase model of radicalization should not be a straitjacket or a conveyor belt.

With this in mind, our own model (see also p. ix), distinguishes between three phases of radicalization: the vulnerability phase, the group phase, and the action phase.[2] These are successive phases; every phase needs to be passed through in order to reach the final phase of action, but they are sufficiently broad to encompass all varieties of radicalization trajectories. While this model is thus not a straitjacket, it is also not a one-size-fits-all model that covers so many processes that it is stretched beyond recognition; it still offers an explanation of the distinctive process of radicalization. The very same phase model also serves as a framework for processes of deradicalization, which will be discussed in Chapter 9.

We will briefly describe these stages subsequently, even though the real proof of the validity of the model can be found in the subsequent chapters. As Moghaddam argued, a model is mainly a way to organize existing psychological knowledge (see also Lygre et al., 2011, p. 609), and so it is up to the remainder of the book to show that this model fits the existing knowledge like a glove.

Vulnerability phase

There are many persons that might potentially be sensitive to radicalization because they are confronted with certain structural conditions: one's socioeconomic position, identification with a group that is perceived to be disadvantaged or discriminated against, or frustration about world affairs. But while such factors – which are often called root factors – might constitute the "background music" to radicalization, Chapter 5 shows that their occurrence is far from sufficient to say that someone is on a path toward radicalization (see also Forest, 2005; Newman, 2006; Schuurman, Bakker, & Eijkman, 2018).

For someone to be truly vulnerable to radicalization, more is needed. Most significantly, he or she must possess a certain "motivational imbalance," where one need is so strong that it dominates others and is conducive to extreme behavior (Kruglanski, Jasko, Chernikova, Dugas, & Webber, 2017). In this context, Chapter 5 will distinguish between justice seekers, identity seekers, significance seekers, and sensation seekers. Such a motivational imbalance can be caused, or worsened, by crucial events in the individual's life; traumatic events such as the death of a loved one, or an experience of discrimination, which we will discuss in Chapter 7 on trigger factors. Relatedly, Chapter 8 shows that an important aspect of resilience against radicalization is the ability to cope with such emotions that are caused by such events.

Group phase

More often than not, what makes individuals vulnerable to radicalization can also make them prone to addiction or more likely to join "deviant" groups like football hooligans or a criminal gang. In other words, they might just as easily end up as a junkie or a gang member. In the context of this book, however, what is relevant is that a radical group can be a viable option to satisfy the vulnerable individual's need for justice, identity, significance, or sensation (see also Horgan, 2008; McCauley & Moskalenko, 2017). Joining such a group is often perhaps more a matter of obtaining these emotional rewards than it is a result of ideological conviction, although of course the individual in question does eventually identify and associate him- or herself with the group's ideals.

The identification with a radical group paves the way toward radicalization, while the subsequent exposure to group-related psychological processes truly propels the individual down this path. Chapter 6 details these processes and describes, among other things, how radical groups enforce a strict division of in- and outgroup, stimulate the experience of negative emotions toward the surrounding society, and psychologically absolve their members of responsibility for violent or other criminal acts. There are also specific triggers (Chapter 7) related to the group phase, which facilitate the transition toward group membership (such as meeting a radical group member or encountering radical propaganda) and consolidate and expedite the radicalization process in this phase (such as burning bridges with those outside the radical group). Radical groups generally tend to force their members to isolate themselves from their surroundings because, as Chapter 8 shows, it is precisely a diverse group membership that – among other things – strengthens the individual's resilience against radicalization.

To be sure, the notion of "group" should be interpreted broadly here, as (violent) radical individuals often also form communities online. But whether they are virtual or physical, or whether they consist of 2 or 2,000 members, groups always play an important role in radicalization processes. Even so-called "lone wolves," after closer inspection, maintain social ties that allow social-psychological processes to come in play and that are essential for the adoption of radical beliefs and the provision of skills training and other means to carry out actual acts of terrorism (Hofmann, 2018; Schuurman et al., 2019).

Action phase

In this phase, the individual is ready to perpetrate violent or other criminal acts on the group's behalf. This can take many forms, depending also on what the law in question designates as criminal behavior. In each case, it could range from prohibited financial and logistic activities – such as aiding terrorist groups or smuggling arms – to direct involvement in terrorist acts (see Taylor & Horgan, 2006; McCauley & Moskalenko, 2017). Interesting to note in this regard is that threats can also be seen as integral part of violent attacks and that some threats, given their impact, may very well also be considered attacks in and of themselves (Brown, 2018).

Such acts can be seen as an extension of the processes pertaining to the group phase, but these cannot be the only relevant factors. After all, earlier this chapter, we already established that this final step toward action demands a very thorough causal explanation. Fortunately, there is a growing body of work that points to distinct factors leading to violence instead of the "mere" adoption of radical beliefs, taking its cue from the observation that there are many radicals and relatively few terrorists. For example, prior experience with violence, either as the victim or the perpetrator, can be a strong predictor of the individual committing acts of violence himself (Crone, 2016; Saramifar, 2018). Resorting to violence is more a matter of imitation, of mentors in the group that have experience with violence (Crone, 2016), or of documented real-life violence in Jihadist videos, for example (Bartlett & Miller 2012). It is a matter of acquiring a skill, which is why participation in a terrorist training camp is one of the most significant triggers that help radicalized individuals transition to the final action phase (see Chapter 7). Yet others point to the complexity of a group's way of thinking— in other words, the degree to which they recognize other ways of thinking – in order to separate violent from non-violent radical groups (Suedfeld, Cross, & Logan, 2013). The latter is also connected to the cognitive aspect of resilience against radicalization (see Chapter 8), which concerns the degree to which the individual is motivated to abstain from black-and-white thinking or needs "cognitive closure" – an aspect of resilience that is also relevant in earlier phases of the radicalization process. All in all, it is safe to say that the step to action merits its own phase in radicalization models, despite the fact that there currently is no definite call on what exactly enables or causes this step.

Conclusion

People do not turn into radicals overnight, let alone *violent* radicals. Instead, radicalization should be seen as a gradual process that extends over a certain amount of time, involving a sequence of events and factors. Earlier phase models provided an overly narrow, rigid, and deterministic view of this process, while other more complex models often lost sight of the sequenced, phased nature of radicalization. A phase model of radicalization should be sufficiently distinctive but also broad and flexible enough to encompass the wide variety of radicalization trajectories. In this chapter, such a model was outlined by distinguishing between the (successive) vulnerability, group, and action phase. These phases will serve as a backdrop that helps order and structure the various factors that will be described in the following chapters.

Endnotes

1. This idea of metaphor conveyor belts was coined by Zeyno Baran in 2004 (see also Glees & Pope, 2005) and has met considerable criticism since then.
2. This is distinction is (roughly) based on the model developed in Doosje et al. (2016).

References

Bartlett, J. & Miller, C. (2012). The edge of violence: Towards telling the difference between violent and non-violent radicalization. *Terrorism and Political Violence*, 24(1), 1–21.

Borum, R. (2011a). Radicalization into violent extremism I: A review of social science theories. *Journal of Strategic Security*, 4(4), 7–36.

Borum, R. (2011b). Radicalization into violent extremism II: A review of conceptual models and empirical research. *Journal of Strategic Security*, 4(4), 37–62.

Brown, J. M. (2018). Force of words: The role of threats in terrorism. *Terrorism and Political Violence*, available at: https://doi.org/10.1080/09546553.2018.1486301

Crone, M. (2016). Radicalization revisited: Violence, politics and the skills of the body. *International Affairs*, 92(3), 587–604

Della Porta, D. (2013). *Clandestine political violence*. Cambridge University Press.

Doosje, B., Moghaddam, F. M., Kruglanski, A. W., Wolf, A., Mann, L., & Feddes, A. R. (2016). Terrorism, radicalization and de-radicalization. *Current Opinion in Psychology*, 11, 79–84.

Forest, J. J. F. (2005). Exploring root causes of terrorism: An introduction. In: J. J. F. Forest (Ed.), *The making of a terrorist, Volume III: Root causes*. Westport/London: Praeger Security International.

Glees, A., & Pope, C. (2005). *When students turn to terror: Terrorist and extremist activity on British campuses*. London: Social Affairs Unit.

Hafez, M., & Mullins, C. (2015). The radicalization puzzle: A theoretical synthesis of empirical approaches to homegrown extremism. *Studies in Conflict & Terrorism*, 38(11), 958–975,

Hofmann, D. C. (2018). How "Alone" are Lone-Actors? Exploring the ideological, signaling, and support networks of lone-actor terrorists. *Studies in Conflict &Terrorism*,

Horgan, J. (2008). From profiles to pathways and roots to routes: Perspectives from psychology on radicalization into terrorism. *The ANNALS of the American Academy of Political and Social Science*, 618(1), 80–94.

Horgan, J. G. (2017). Psychology of terrorism: Introduction to the special issue. *American Psychologist*, 72(3), 199–204.

King, M., & Taylor, D. M. (2011). The radicalization of home grown Jihadists. A review of theoretical models and social psychological evidence. *Terrorism and Political Violence*, 23, 602–622.

Kruglanski, A. W., Jasko, K., Chernikova, M., Dugas, M., & Webber, D. (2017). To the fringe and back: Violent extremism and the psychology of deviance. *American Psychologist*, 72(3), 217–230.

Lygre, R. B., Eid, J., Larsson, G., & Ranstorp, M. (2011). Terrorism as a process: A critical review of Moghaddam's "Staircase to Terrorism". *Scandinavian Journal of Psychology* 52(6), 609–616.

McCauley, C., & Moskalenko, S. (2008). Mechanisms of political radicalization: Pathways toward terrorism. *Terrorism and Political Violence*, 20(3), 415–433.

McCauley, C., & Moskalenko, S. (2011). *Friction: How radicalization happens to them and us.* Oxford.

McCauley, C., & Moskalenko, S. (2017). Understanding political radicalization: The two-pyramids model. *American Psychologist,* 72(3), 205–216.

Moghaddam, F. M. (2005). The staircase to terrorism: A psychological exploration. *American Psychologist,* 60(2), 161–169.

Neumann, P. R. (2013). The trouble with radicalization. *International Affairs,* 89(4), July 2013, 873–893.

Newman, E. (2006). Exploring the "Root Causes" of Terrorism. *Studies in Conflict & Terrorism,* 29, 749–772.

Precht, T. (2007). Home grown terrorism and Islamist radicalization in Europe: From conversion to terrorism. *Danish Ministry of Defense,* December 2007, available at: http://www.justitsministeriet.dk

Sageman, M. (2008). A strategy for fighting international Islamist terrorists. *The Annals of the American Academy of Political and Social Science,* 618, 223–231.

Saramifar Y. (2018). Pursuing the allure of combat: An ethnography of violence amongst Iraqi Shi'i combatants fighting ISIS. *Critical Studies on Terrorism,* 12(2), 210–227.

Schuurman, B., Lindekilde, L., Malthaner, S., O'Connor, F., Gill, P., & Bouhana, N. (2019). End of the lone wolf: The typology that should not have been. *Studies in Conflict & Terrorism,* 42(8), 771–778,

Schuurman, B. W., Bakker, E., & Eijkman, Q. (2018) Structural influences on involvement in European homegrown jihadism: A case study. *Terrorism and Political Violence,* 30(1), 97–115.

Silber, M. D., & Bhatt, A. (2007). *Radicalization in the West: The homegrown threat.* New York: Police Department.

Suedfeld, P., Cross, M. R. W., & Logan, M. C. (2013). Can thematic content analysis separate the pyramid of ideas from the pyramid of action? A comparison among different degrees of commitment to violence. White Paper. Retrieved 14 December 2015 from: http://www.researchgate.net

Taylor, M., & Horgan, J. G. (2006). A conceptual framework for addressing psychological process in the development of the terrorist. *Terrorism and Political Violence,* 18(4), 585–601.

Veldhuis T., & Staun, J. (2009). *Islamist radicalisation: A root cause model.* The Hague: Netherlands Institute of International Relations Clingendael.

Wiktorowicz, Q. (2005). *Radical Islam rising: Muslim extremism in the West.* Lanham, MD: Rowman & Littlefield Publishers, Inc.

Chapter 5

Wanted: Radical

About profiles, populations, and personalities

Goals

- Discusses the role of age, gender, and socioeconomic status in regard to radicalization.
- Reviews the role of psychopathology, behavioral disorders, and personality.
- Gives an overview of different psychological needs that play a role in radicalization processes.

Introduction

On July 22, 2011, a bomb exploded in Oslo, Norway, killing eight persons. On the same day, as described in Chapter 1, Anders Breivik shot and killed 69 young individuals on the island Utøya. Breivik was caught alive and brought to trial. Whenever such terrorist attacks take place and people start searching for the reason behind the act, there is a risk of the perpetrator becoming a personification of all terrorists – especially since such attacks are very rare. A recurring theme in the study of radicalization and terrorism is whether all terrorists are "crazy." In this chapter, we look into this and other characteristics that may or may not typify radical individuals. Are radicals crazy? Are they male or female? Rich or poor? Well educated or not? Subsequently, we will first look into these questions and then discuss a different way to look at which individuals may feel attracted to extremism, namely the role of psychological needs.

Gender, age, education, IQ, and marital status

Gender and age

There is overall consensus in the literature that young men dominate extremist groups. However, (young) women certainly are not absent in extremist groups. For example, between 2012 and 2015, an estimated 4,000 European citizens of

Muslim origin (or converts to Islam) traveled to Syria to join forces that fought against the regime of Bashar al Assad (Bakker & De Leede, 2015). The German Federal Police kept record of 784 German residents who traveled to Syria until June 2016 (Bundes Kriminal Amt, 2016). While men were overrepresented (79%), a significant number of these foreign travelers (21%) were female. A look at Dutch police databases, which included 140 foreign travelers in 2014 (Weenink, 2015), also shows that whereas the majority was male (84%), females were also present (16%). If we look at the average age, it seems that radical people mainly are to be found in adolescence until young adulthood (about 15–30 years old). For example, while some of the Dutch foreign fighters were adolescents, the mean age at the time of leaving was 25.8 years. The largest age group was between 22 and 25 (322 persons, 41%).

A similar picture arises in right-wing extremist groups, which are also dominated by young men in their adolescence or early adulthood (Rippl & Seipel, 1999; Van der Valk & Wagenaar, 2010). These are all radicals in groups. The gender division may be different for lone-actor terrorists (individuals who threaten to use violence or commit violent acts without any direct support of others). Recently, De Roy van Zuijdewijn and Bakker (2016) examined personal characteristics of lone-actor terrorists in the EU between 2000 and 2015. The population studied included right-wing extremists, left-wing extremists, and "school shooters." They reported that almost all lone-actor terrorists in the EU were men (96%), with an average age of 29.7 years old.

The fact that extremist scenes are overrepresented by young men may reflect the nature of activities of these organizations, which are usually dominated by men (e.g., politics, public demonstrations, violent behavior). The relatively large presence of men also explains that little research has focused on the case of female terrorism – even though women have been present in most terrorist organizations, including right-wing extremist groups, Islamic extremist groups, left-wing extremist groups (such as the Red Brigade in the 1970s and the FARC - Fuerzas Armadas Revolucionarias de Colombia - in Columbia), and so on (Cunningham, 2007; Bloom, 2016). A quite well-known example of female terrorism is the so-called "Black Widows" group in Chechnya, see Box 5.1.

In 2014–2015, there were at least a few hundred Western women in the areas controlled by the extremist group "Islamic State" (IS) (Bakker & De Leede, 2015). The demographics of these women varied greatly, with some girls as young as 15. Some were highly educated, others had a low IQ. Some had a troubled childhood, others came from stable families. Some had strong convictions, while others were described as impressionable. Motivations of these women did not seem to differ that much from those of men traveling to Syria to join IS. Reasons for joining reportedly were repression of Muslims worldwide, a religious duty to support

Box 5.1   The Black Widows as a case study of female terrorism

An often-mentioned example of female terrorists are the so-called Black Widows, also called *Shahidka* (female martyrs). The Black Widows, a name given by the Russian media (see also Nivat, 2005), have been held responsible for several terrorist attacks, of which the most famous was the hostage situation in the Dubrovka theater in Moscow in 2002 (168 people were killed) and the hostages taken in a school in Beslan in 2004 (334 children and adults were killed). The women were part of a Chechen group who rebelled against the "occupation" of Chechen territory by the Russian Federal Army. Anne Nivat (2005) interviewed the mother of one of the assailants of the Dubrovka attack, who said her daughter was driven by "despair" and a quest for *significance* in life. By sacrificing their lives, they could gain a place in paradise. Nivat also pointed out that *injustice* played an important role in relation to the Russian "occupation" (most of the female assailants were widows of rebels killed in the Russian-Chechen war in 1999–2000). The conflict also provided an opportunity to build their *identity* as being faithful young Muslims. As we will see at the end of this chapter, these psychological motivations - a need for *identity*, *justice*, *significance*, and *sensation* - are often present in radicalizing individuals.

jihad, an appealing idea of a fresh start, the feeling of not belonging in the society where they grew up, and a sense of adventure.

Perhaps a more interesting question than the number of women in extremist groups is the role they may play in the group. Women in terrorist groups generally are the supporters of male fighters. They facilitate the functioning of the organization (carrying messages, taking care of financial issues) and educate children in the ideology. Compared to men, women are less expected to be suicide terrorists. But if they do commit a terrorist suicide act, it is likely to draw even more media attention because females are stereotyped as nonviolent in many societies (Von Knop, 2007). Particularly interesting is the role as "terrorist cover girl," where females become propaganda material for the extremist group (Bloom, 2016).

An example of the responsible role women can have in terrorist groups is the Dutch Tanja Nijmeijer. She joined the FARC in Columbia in 2002 as a revolutionary and ultimately became known as a negotiator with the Columbian government on behalf of the group. Pictures and descriptions of her past were widespread in the media (see also Figure 5.1).

A specific case of female radicalization that attracted quite some media attention were the Bethnal Green school girls (Bennhold, August 17, 2015). It concerned three London girls who were at the time 15 and 16 years old. The girls radicalized

Figure 5.1 Women are present in most terrorist organizations. Some become role models and serve representative functions, such as Tanja Nijmeijer, a Dutch woman who became a negotiator for the FARC in Columbia. (Photo by Manuel Paz (2016). Retrieved from: https://nl.wikipedia.org/wiki/Tanja_Nijmeijer#/media/Bestand:Tanja_Nijmeijer_(2016).jpg.)

via the internet and social media by online recruiters of IS. They traveled in 2014 to Syria to join the extremist group. Western women who joined IS were excluded from the frontline battles but mainly served to support male warriors and facilitate the functioning of the organization (i.e., providing finances, contacting females over social media).

So, while young men dominate extremist groups, women and girls are also present, and each may fulfill particular gender related roles in the organization.

Marital status

No consistent pattern exists in regard to marital status. Sageman (2004) reported that 70% of the 400 terrorists he analyzed were married. The earlier mentioned dataset of the Bundes Kriminal Amt (2016) included information about the marital status on 688 foreign fighters. About half of this group was married, 28% was married according to German law, and 22% were married according to Islamic rites. About 42% of these individuals were known to have children at the time of departure. In addition, in an interview study with 12 former right-wing extremists, Van der Valk and Wagenaar (2010) did not find marriage an important factor in explaining why individuals joined right-wing extremist groups.

Research by criminologists points out that marriage can be a turning point in a criminal career. Getting married is the starting point of a positive turn away from crime among both men and women (Sampson & Laub, 1992; Bersani et al., 2009) and makes young criminal gang members become less involved in the group (Tripp, 2007). For radicalization, however, this may work differently. There are several cases known where women actually married into extremist groups (De Graaf, 2012). However, thus far, there is no consistent evidence that marriage plays a particularly important role in the radicalization process (or in the deradicalization process, for that matter).

Education and poverty

With regard to education, there is also no clear picture to paint. For example, the earlier mentioned study by the German Federal Police on 784 German residents who traveled to Syria reports data on education level for 289 travelers (Bundes Kriminal Amt, 2016). A significant number (86%) had completed secondary school, 7% had other school-leaving certificates, and 7% did not complete secondary school. Ninety-four (32%) individuals had started their university studies before leaving Germany, but only 10% had completed their studies at point of departure. In another study among Al-Qaeda militants in the 1980s, Sageman (2004) concluded that "three fourths" were of higher social economic status. Later waves of young individuals who joined the group in the 1990s typically had a lower education and were called the "terrorist wannabes." These young individuals joined the group out of anger and frustration and were partly motivated by a need for adventure and heroism.

Research comparing "regular" criminals with prisoners convicted for terrorism in the Netherlands shows that both groups have relatively low education levels and high drop-out rates (Versteegt et al., 2018). However, an open question remains whether these lower education levels were the result of the radicalization process or the cause.

Historically, a mixed picture of education is found in far-left terrorism (Weinberg & Eubank, 1988). For right-wing extremists, lower-educated individuals do seem to be overrepresented, and having higher education reportedly decreases the likelihood of involvement in extremist groups (Willems, 1995; Boehnke et al., 1998).

The level of education may be related to the *type of terrorist*. For example, socially "frustrated youths" who radicalize based on experiences of being treated unfairly (i.e., based on discrimination or unfair competition with others over economic resources) are typically individuals with limited education and those who suffer from unemployment and economic hardship. These frustrated youths may be contrasted with ideologists who embrace ideologies through education and are often well educated (Bjørgo, 2011). Another distinction that can be made is whether we are dealing with leaders, who may have a higher education, or followers, who may have a lower education. In that sense, education may be a predictor of the role an individual fulfils in a terrorist organization.

Poverty has little to do with terrorism is the conclusion of Krueger and Malecková (2003). Based on a study among 129 Hezbollah militants over the past 20 years, they conclude that "[a]ny connection between poverty, education and terrorism is indirect, complicated and probably quite weak" (p. 119).

The relation between socioeconomic status and radicalization is likely to depend to a large extent on (perceived) inequality in a society. Participation in a terrorist group is greater in societies that are unequal (i.e., large differences in economic wealth) compared to more egalitarian societies (Lee, 2011). On top of that, the more inequality is perceived, the stronger the feeling of being treated unjustly. This so-called "relative deprivation" is considered a root factor of radicalization (Moghaddam, 2005) and will be further discussed in Chapter 6, where we discuss group factors of radicalization.

In sum, when looking at the role of education and poverty, a mixed picture arises. It may depend on the period in which individuals radicalize, and there may be a relation with particular types of radicals (socially frustrated person versus ideologist; leaders versus followers). Instead of making statements about whether these factors play a role, it seems more beneficial to examine how the *content* of education (i.e., teaching youngsters about democracy, former radicals who serve as role models warning young people against extremist groups) and whether a *positive outlook on employment* may serve as a protective factors against radicalization.

Psychopathology, behavioral disorders, and personality

Is there a connection between mental and behavioral disorders, personality, and terrorist involvement? This question has occupied researchers on terrorism for decades (Horgan, 2003; Sageman, 2004; Victoroff, 2005; Gill & Corner, 2017). For example, in "Psychopath as Terrorist," Cooper concludes that "while it is not necessary to be a psychopath in order to be a terrorist – it helps." (1978, p. 261). Silke (1998, p. 52) named the continuously recurring theme of terrorist abnormality the Cheshire-cat logic, using "Alice In Wonderland" as a metaphor: The cat believes only mad people could inhabit Wonderland, so consequently anyone you meet there *must* be mad! The discussion on the role of psychopathology in radicalization keeps reappearing, as illustrated in Box 5.2.

Overall, the evidence for a link between psychopathology and terrorism is very weak. The existing body of evidence pointing out radicals' *normality* is larger and of better empirical quality (Schulten, Doosje, Spaaij, & Kamphuis, 2019; Silke, 1998; Victoroff, 2005). Nevertheless, review studies show that mental disorders are definitely not absent among individuals who radicalized. This may be particularly important in the case of lone-actor terrorists. For example, De Roy van Zuijdewijn and Bakker (2016) conclude that of the 120 perpetrators in the EU between 2000 and 2015, 35% suffered from a mental disorder.

Box 5.2   The psychiatric evaluation of Anders Breivik

As described in the opening paragraph of this chapter, Anders Breivik was sub-
jected to a series of intensive forensic evaluations (see Bjørgo, de Graaf, van der
Heide, Hemmingby, & Weggemans, 2016, Melle (2013) and Wessely, 2012
for detailed discussions). In the trial, the judges had to determine whether
Breivik could be held accountable for his deeds. Four psychiatrists conducted
two subsequent forensic evaluations. In the first evaluation, two psychiatrists
used a combination of unstructured dialogues in combination with structured
diagnostic interviews. As a basis, they used the DSM-IV, the diagnostic manual
that is used by psychiatrists and psychologists to determine psychopathologi-
cal disorders in individuals. On November 29, 2011, the psychiatrists judged
that Breivik suffered from schizophrenia. They based their diagnosis on the
bizarre and grandiose images Breivik suffered from. These included viewing
Islam as a threat and his ideas to improve the gene pool of the Norwegians.
One way of doing so was to create special settlements for Norwegians (not
for immigrants!). Taken aside, the absurdness of his notions (and the fact that
there surely are those who agree with them) and the meticulous preparation
of his deeds do not fit the disorganized behavior that comes along with schizophrenia. The verdict was important, as it implied diminished responsibility
for Breivik and probably admission to a secure hospital facility. However, a
second psychiatric assessment was ordered by the judges as a number of highly
regarded experts in forensic psychiatry and psychology found the first assessment mistaken on several counts. There was also severe criticism from experts
on rightwing extremism and terrorism that the psychiatric team had disre-
garded Breivik's ideological worldview and role as a terrorist and, due to that,
(mis) interpreted many of his statements and paranoid delusions. These criticisms from a broad range of experts were so serious that they undermined the
legitimacy of the verdict finding Breivik "not guilty" and convicted to psychiatric treatment based on the first psychiatric assessment. Therefore, a second
opinion was called for by the judges. The relative weight of the two psychiatric assessments was carefully treated during the trial and in the verdict. The
judges ultimately found the second assessment more convincing.

In the Dutch police database including 140 Dutch foreign fighters, 6% had diagnosed
disorders, including psychotic disorder, narcissistic disorder, attention-deficit/
hyperactivity disorder, schizophrenia, autism spectrum, and PTSD. It was found that
20% of the sample had indications of mental health problems (Weenink, 2015).

While some radical individuals may suffer from mental disorders, it cannot
be concluded that mental disorders cause by definition radicalization and lead to
terrorist acts. It is often unclear whether a specific mental disorder is in fact related to
violence (Wessely, 2012). In a recent review of the literature on the relation between

mental disorders and terrorism over the past 40 years, Gill and Corner (2017) point out that instead of giving a "yes" or "no" answer to this question, there should be room for nuance. Rather than saying that there are (no) terrorists who are psychopaths or narcissists, it should be said that "it is too simple (and unsupported) to suggest these factors caused the initial engagement with terrorism alone" (p. 233). In answering this question, it should be specified which specific disorder is focused on as well as what type of terrorism (i.e., group-based terrorism or lone-actor terrorists).

The findings reviewed previously have important consequences for risk assessment. Individual characteristics may play a role in radicalization processes, but what role and under which circumstances is unclear due to the mixed evidence or, if available, weak empirical evidence. Reviews of the available empirical evidence show quite clearly that there is no sufficient evidence that allows for risk assessment of radicalization or terrorism based on individual characteristics (Dernevik et al., 2009; Feddes, 2017). Instead, it may be more useful to focus on the underlying psychological needs of individuals.

Psychological needs

In order to prevent violent radicalization, it is important to understand what drives an individual to join an extremist group and to use violence. As depicted at the bottom of the theoretical model on p. ix, each terrorist may have a unique *psychological need* that forms the underlying motivation for why he or she radicalizes. Identifying this need will be useful in determining how best to approach this individual in interventions. Needs are important, as they can motivate us to behave in a certain manner. Psychologists have long studied how motivation is related to behavior. For example, Abraham Maslow (1970) proposed five different human needs, which can be arranged in a hierarchy, where the basic needs need to be fulfilled before a person will spend time and energy on the "higher" needs. From the bottom (with the basic existential needs) to the top, these are: (1) *physiological needs* (the minimal requirements for life such as food and water), (2) *safety needs* (being protected from danger from the environment), (3) *attachment needs* (being accepted by others), (4) *esteem needs* (feeling competent, feeling respected by others and the self), and (5) *self-actualization needs* (playing, exploring). Needs are important because if our needs are not met, we are motivated to do something about it. In other words, needs give us a direction in life. In the literature on processes of radicalization, four needs can be distinguished that overlap with several of Maslow's needs (see also Macdougall, van der Veen, Feddes, Nickolson, & Doosje, 2018).

Identity seekers

Groups provide us with *safety* and *attachment* and are an important source of *self-esteem*. According to social identity theory (Tajfel & Turner, 1979), a person's sense of who they are depends to a large extent on to which social groups they belong to. This so-called *social identity* is particularly important, as it can boost our self-esteem (when we belong to a successful and important social group) or lower our self-esteem (if we belong to a social group that is stigmatized or frowned upon). As with any social group, an extremist group can be attractive to a person, as it can provide them with safety, attachment, and self-esteem. In an interview study with 13 former right-wing individuals, we investigated the reported levels of self-esteem before, during, and after they were member of an extremist group (Feddes et al., 2013). The results showed that before joining, levels of self-esteem were generally low; during membership self-esteem was high; and after leaving the group, individuals generally experienced low levels of self-esteem again. Indeed, some individuals reported to have "fallen in a black void" after leaving the group, as they had to distance themselves from their friends who were all members. So, whereas joining an extremist group can be attractive to fulfill the identity need, leaving an extremist group may be less attractive, as it implies losing the protection, attachment, and self-esteem one is looking for (Bjørgo, 1997; Van der Valk & Wagenaar, 2010).

Another example is the establishment of the Caliphate by IS in July 2014. The establishment of such a successful and powerful group resulted in an increase in foreign travelers joining IS (Bundes Kriminal Amt, 2016). Often these were young adolescents who were part of ethnic groups that are discriminated against and who feel disconnected from the society they live in (Doosje et al., 2012, 2013; Van Bergen et al., 2015). The sudden appearance of a strong group such as IS formed an excellent opportunity to fulfill the basic need to belong to a successful group.

A threat to our identity may also feed into further radicalization, as the Breivik case illustrated (see also Box 5.2). A distinction can be made between *realistic threat*, which refers to a perceived threat of loss of materialistic resources (for example, one's job) and *symbolic threat*, which refers to a threat to one's culture or identity (Stephan & Stephan, 2000). Individuals who feel a realistic or symbolic threat are also more likely to approve ideology-based violence (Doosje et al., 2012, 2013). In interviews with former right-wing extremists, out-group threat was found to be an important predictor for the decision to join an extremist group. This is illustrated by the following statement of a male participant in the Netherlands (Feddes et al., 2013, p. 49):

> Well, that was a turning point as I would name it. That was pretty clear for me. I will always remember it. I was a student at secondary school and one day I was sitting behind the computer and was looking outside. There I saw a playground in the middle of some buildings where I was raised since I was four years old. There were some Somali children playing, with a headscarf and so on. Then a Dutch girl came who wanted to join them but she was beaten and chased away. That was the point for me. Then I turned to the computer and typed the words 'White Power'.

For this individual, this incident was an example of a threat to his group (in this case, the Dutch, whom he felt were threatened by immigrant out-groups), which increased his motivation to join a right-wing extremist group. Joining a group may, in that respect, also be a way to deal with (perceived) danger from the environment.

The need for a positive identity may be dependent on age. The developmental psychologist Erik Erikson (1968) termed adolescence as "a time of storm and stress." In this age period, people are particularly concerned about who they are and to which groups they belong. Adolescents may, therefore, be particularly susceptible to propaganda that aims at identity needs.

Justice seekers

Some individuals may be particularly attracted to extremist groups to counter injustice done toward themselves or their social group. Many extremist groups have this element of injustice fitted into their ideology. Muslim extremist groups may emphasize they fight against injustice done to Muslims, right-wing extremist groups may want to defend the rights of the white "superior" race, left-wing extremist groups may want to fight for social equality, and so on. Extremist groups can be very attractive to justice seekers, as they provide tools and social support to fight perceived injustice.

Feelings of injustice and relative deprivation have been identified as so-called "root factors of radicalization" (Moghaddam, 2005; Venhaus, 2010; Schmid, 2013; Van den Bos, 2018). *Relative deprivation* is a feeling of injustice that involves a comparison with your own living standard in the past, with others, or with other groups. It is the feeling that people have when they as an individual or as a group find they are less well off than they consider being just and deserved (Crosby, 1976; Grant & Brown, 1995). These feelings can be based on economic conditions but are also related to political, cultural and religious issues. Importantly, feelings of deprivation have been shown to be associated with more positive attitudes toward the use of ideology-based violence (Doosje et al., 2012, 2013). These feelings need not be limited to the country one lives in. For example, through strong identification with other Muslims throughout the world, radical Muslims may experience their group to be the victim of suppression by the United States, Western countries, or non-Muslims in general. An excerpt from interviews with radical Islamic youth held by Buijs and colleagues (2006) can illustrate this (p. 176):

> I am also worried about suppression of Muslims. I feel with my religious brothers. Islam is like a body; the pain is felt through all parts. I therefore feel the pain of Muslims.

Feelings of injustice can result in negative emotions and thereby also in radicalization (Van den Bos, 2018). Experienced anger, frustration, hatred, and humiliation as a result of feelings of injustice are important factors that are at the background of radicalization (Moghaddam, 2005; Feddes et al., 2012). These emotions can play a role at the individual level (for example, you are angry because of what someone did to you as a person) as well as the group level (anger because of what someone did to members of your group). At the group level, fear, anger, contempt, hate, and humiliation are mentioned as motivating group-based retribution and revenge (e.g., Lickel, 2012).

In sum, feelings of being treated unjustly can be a powerful drive to join extremist groups. Besides identity and injustice, the basic need to have a sense of meaning in life is a third need that may motivate individuals to do so.

Significance seekers

The need for significance is considered a dominant motivator for radicalization (Kruglanski et al., 2018). It is related to Maslow's need of having a positive self-worth. Radicalization can be a result of re-establishing a sense of significance, for example, when you lose face (after having been insulted) or experience a strong setback in life. For example, negative experiences at school or at home are often mentioned as reasons for joining extremist right-wing groups (Möller & Schuhmacher, 2006; Van der Valk & Wagenaar, 2010). *Humiliation* is a particularly interesting emotion in this respect. In numerous "school shootings" in the United States, humiliating bullying of the perpetrator was mentioned as a driving factor (Leary et al., 2003). Humiliating or denigrating experiences, but also traumatic experiences (such as a confrontation with death), may result in feelings of deep uncertainty about one's place in the world, a state that is called "existential uncertainty" (Van den Bos, 2009). As a result, individuals may start derogating out-groups that are perceived as threatening their view of the world. Indeed, experimental work has shown that when individuals think about their own death, they denigrate threatening out-groups more and also show greater support for violent acts against these groups (Pyszczynski et al., 2006).

Experienced humiliation has also been related to (suicide) terrorism (Lindner, 2001; Fontan, 2006; Cook & Allison, 2007; Fattah & Fierke, 2009; Kruglanski et al., 2009; Rice, 2009). Appeals to humiliation have been used as a rhetorical tool by extremist leaders to instigate hate and revenge against other groups and to justify acts of terrorism (see also the reference to humiliations by Osama Bin Laden described in Chapter 6). Indeed, field research (among extremist prisoners in the Philippines and Sri Lanka) and laboratory experiments have shown that individuals who experience humiliation experience a stronger need for certainty and psychological closure and thereby become more supportive of terrorism (Webber et al., 2018). Thinking back of Maslow's theory of motivation, significance seeking seems to be strongly related to Maslow's need of esteem.

Sensation seekers

Sensation seeking relates to Maslow's dimension of self-actualization, where adventure and play are key elements. Sensation seekers are those who are typically on the lookout for excitement and adventure, and these persons may be particularly attracted to radical groups (Nussio, 2017). Bjørgo and Carlsson (2005) call these individuals the "thrill seekers" and posit that this need is key for many individuals who join right-wing extremist groups. Feeling attracted to violence can play a role in the decision to join the extreme scene (Van der Valk & Wagenaar, 2010). Indeed, extremist groups target the need for sensation in their publication campaigns by using pictures of tough-looking warriors and the promise of adventure (Van San, 2015). While these images mainly put men at the center (but note that there are also images of female fighters; see also the earlier mentioned case of Tanja Nijmeijer), the need for sensation is not only relevant for men. The possibility of marrying and supporting a fighter is also sometimes used to attract radical females (Sageman, 2008). In line with this, Hall (2015, April 18) describes the case of a 20-year-old American girl who traveled to Syria to become an "IS-bride."

The need for sensation may also come about from simple boredom when not much is happening in life and there is no positive outlook that things will be better in the future, in combination with an attraction to, arms, violence, and excitement (Venhaus, 2010; Crone, 2016), for example, in the case of unemployment or having a job without prospects. Glory, thrills, and romance may then form important motivators to meet the need for sensation or, in Maslow's terms, the need for *self-actualization*: realizing one's full self, dreams, and capabilities.

It is important to note that the four needs distinguished can overlap and do not necessarily exclude each other. Also, there may be other needs that can be distinguished. More research is needed to get more insight into which and how different needs are at work in radicalization. The idea we pose here is that identifying a particular need is useful in understanding an individual's motivation to radicalize and thereby may be more effective in deradicalizing them.

Conclusion

What has become clear in this chapter is that no specific *WANTED profile* of "the radical" exists. But that does not mean we cannot say anything about the *population* of radical individuals – and the degree to which they generally possess certain characteristics – as well as their *personalities* in the sense of characteristic psychological needs. As Hegghammer (2016) put it in regard to the poverty-terrorism link:

> The causal effect, if there is one, is likely probabilistic, not categorical, meaning that it predisposes for radicalization, in the same way that smoking predisposes you to cancer without guaranteeing that you get it.

Instead of asking whether terrorists are male or female, married or not, young or old, highly educated or not, it is more helpful to ask questions such as: What attracts young men or women to extremist groups? How can marriage or education serve as protective factors against radicalization, or could these factors actually lead to further radicalization? Instead of focusing on the simple dichotomic questions, it may be more fruitful to focus more on the *why* than on the *if*. Understanding the psychological needs of the individual person is helpful as a starting point to counter the radicalization process. In that sense, we can learn from extremist groups who in their propaganda clearly focus on needs such as belonging, injustice, significance, and sensation, as we will see in Chapter 6.

Recommended reading

Gill, P., & Corner, E. (2017). There and back again: The study of mental disorder and terrorist involvement. *American Psychologist*, 72(3), 231.

In this article, Paul Gill and Emily Corner review the past 40 years of research on the relationship between mental disorders and terrorist involvement. They describe four research approaches that can generally be distinguished and give recommendations for future research which, they argue, should move away from simple dichotomous explanations.

References

Bakker, E., & de Leede, S. (2015). *European female Jihadists in Syria: Exploring an under-researched topic*. International Centre for Counter-terrorism. Retrieved from: http://www.icct.nl

Bersani, B. E., Laub, J. H., & Nieuwbeerta, P. (2009). Marriage and desistance from crime in the Netherlands: Do gender and socio-historical context matter? *Journal of Quantitative Criminology*, 25, 3–24.

Bjørgo, T. (1997). *Racist and right-wing violence in Scandinavia: Patterns, perpetrators and responses*. Tano Aschehoug.

Bjørgo, T. (2011). Dreams and disillusionment: Engagement in and disengagement from militant extremist groups. *Crime, Law and Social Change*, 55(4), 277–285.

Bjørgo, T., & Carlsson, Y. (2005). *Early intervention with violent and racist youth groups*. Norwegian Institute of International Affairs. Retrieved from: https://brage.bibsys.no

Bjørgo, T., de Graaf, B., van der Heide, L., Hemmingby, C., & Weggemans, D. (2016). Performing justice, coping with trauma: The trial of Anders Breivik. In Beatrice de Graaf & Alex P. Schmid (Eds.) *"Terrorists on trial. A performative perspective"*, pp. 457-502, Leiden: Leiden University Press.

Bloom, M. (2016). The changing nature of women in extremism and political violence. *Freedom from Fear*, 11, 40–54.

Boehnke, K., Hagan, J., & Merkens, H. (1998). Right – wing extremism among German adolescents: Risk factors and protective factors. *Applied Psychology*, 47, 109–126.

Buijs, F. J., Demant, F., & Hamdy, A. (2006). *Strijders van eigen bodem: Radicale en democratische moslims in Nederland [Home-grown warriors: Radical and democratic Muslims in the Netherland]*. Amsterdam: Amsterdam University Press.

Bundes Kriminal Amt (BKA; Federal Criminal Police Office), BfV (Federal Office for the Protection of the Constitution), HKE (Hesse Information and Competence Centre Against Extremism) (2016). Analysis of the background and process of radicalization among persons who left Germany to travel to Syria or Iraq based on Islamist motivation. Retrieved from: https://www.bka.de

Cook, D., & Allison, O. (2007). *Understanding and addressing suicide attacks: The faith and politics of martyrdom operations*. Greenwood Publishing Group.

Crone, M. (2016). Radicalization revisited: Violence, politics and the skills of the body. *International Affairs*, 92(3), 587–604.

Crosby, F. (1976). A model of egoistical relative deprivation. *Psychological Review*, 83(2), 85.

Cunningham, K. J. (2007) Countering Female Terrorism. *Studies in Conflict & Terrorism*, 30, 113–129.

De Graaf, B. A. (2012). *Gevaarlijke vrouwen. Tien militante vrouwen in het vizier [Dangerous females. A focus on ten militant women]*. Amsterdam: Boom.

Dernevik, M., Beck, A., Grann, M., Hogue, T., & McGuire, J. (2009). The use of psychiatric and psychological evidence in the assessment of terrorist offenders. *The Journal of Forensic Psychiatry & Psychology*, 20(4), 508–515.

De Roy van Zuijdewijn, J., & Bakker, E. (2016). Analysing personal characteristics of Lone-Actor terrorists: Research findings and recommendations. *Perspectives on Terrorism*, 10(2), 42–49.

Doosje, B., Loseman, A., & Van den Bos, K. (2013). Determinants of radicalization of Islamic youth in the Netherlands: Personal uncertainty, perceived injustice, and perceived group threat. *Journal of Social Issues*, 69(3), 586–604.

Doosje, B., Van den Bos, K., Loseman, A., Feddes, A. R., & Mann, L. (2012). "My In-group is Superior!": Susceptibility for Radical Right-wing Attitudes and Behaviors in Dutch Youth. *Negotiation and Conflict Management Research*, 5(3), 253–268.

Erikson, E. H. (1968). *Identity, youth, and crisis* (1st ed.). New York: Norton.

Fattah, K., & Fierke, K. M. (2009). A clash of emotions: The politics of humiliation and political violence in the Middle East. *European Journal of International Relations*, 15(1), 67–93.

Feddes, A. R. (2017). Risk assessment in integral security policy. In: L. Colaert (Ed.), *"Deradicalization": Scientific insights for a Flemish policy* (pp. 49–64). Brussels: Vlaams Vredesinstituut.

Feddes, A. R., Mann, L., & Doosje, B. (2012). From extreme emotions to extreme actions: Explaining non-normative collective action and reconciliation. *Behavioral and Brain Sciences*, 35(6), 432–433.

Feddes, A. R., Mann, L., & Doosje, B. (2013). *Scientific approach to formulate indicators and responses to radicalisation: Empirical study*. Amsterdam: University of Amsterdam.

Fontan, V. (2006). Polarization between occupier and occupied in post-Saddam Iraq: Colonial humiliation and the formation of political violence. *Terrorism and Political Violence*, 18(2), 217–238.

Gill, P., & Corner, E. (2017). There and back again: The study of mental disorder and terrorist involvement. *American Psychologist*, 72(3), 231.

Grant, P. R., & Brown, R. (1995). From ethnocentrism to collective protest: Responses to relative deprivation and threats to social identity. *Social Psychology Quarterly*, 58(3), 195.

Hall, E. (2015, 18 April). Gone girl: An interview with an American in ISIS. Retrieved from: http://www.buzzfeed.com

Hegghammer, T. (2016). Revisiting the poverty-terrorism link in European jihadism. Paper presented at *the Society for Terrorism Research Annual Conference*, Leiden University, Leiden, the Netherlands, November 8.

Horgan, J. G. (2003). The Search for the Terrorist Personality. In: A. Silke (Ed.), *Terrorists, victims and society: Psychological perspectives on terrorism and its consequences*. Chichester, UK: John Wiley & Sons.

Krueger, A. B., & Malečková, J. (2003). Education, poverty and terrorism: Is there a causal connection? *Journal of Economic perspectives*, 17, 119–144.

Kruglanski, A., Jasko, K., Webber, D., Chernikova, M., & Molinario, E. (2018). The making of violent extremists. *Review of General Psychology*, 22(1), 107–120.

Kruglanski, A. W., Chen, X., Dechesne, M., Fishman, S., & Orehek, E. (2009). Fully committed: Suicide bombers' motivation and the quest for personal significance. *Political Psychology*, 30(3), 331–357.

Leary, M. R., Kowalski, R. M., Smith, L., & Phillips, S. (2003). Teasing, rejection, and violence: Case studies of the school shootings. *Aggressive Behavior: Official Journal of the International Society for Research on Aggression*, 29(3), 202–214.

Lee, A. (2011). Who becomes a terrorist?: Poverty, education, and the origins of political violence. *World Politics*, 63, 203–245.

Lickel, B. (2012). Retribution and revenge. In L. R. Tropp (Ed.), *Oxford library of psychology. The Oxford handbook of intergroup conflict* (pp. 89–105). New York, NY, US: Oxford University Press.

Lindner, E. G. (2001). Humiliation as the source of terrorism: A new paradigm. *Peace Research*, 33(2), 59–68.

Macdougall, A. I., Van der Veen, J., Feddes, A. R., Nickolson, L., & Doosje, B. (2018). Different strokes for different folks: the role of psychological needs and other risk factors in early radicalisation. *International Journal of Developmental Science*, 12, 37–50.

Maslow, A. H. (1970). *Motivation and Personality*. New York: Harper & Row.

Melle, I. (2013). The Breivik case and what psychiatrists can learn from it. *World Psychiatry*, 12, 16–21.

Moghaddam, F. M. (2005). The staircase to terrorism: A psychological exploration. *American Psychologist*, 60(2), 161.

Möller, K., & Schuhmacher, N. (2006). *Rechte Glatzen: Rechtsextreme Orientierungs-und Szenezusammenhänge-Einstiegs-, Verbleibs-und Ausstiegsprozesse von Skinheads [Rightwing orientation and entry, membership and exit from Skinnheads]*. Springer-Verlag.

Nivat, A. (2005). The black widows: Chechen women join the Fight for Independence— and Allah. *Studies in Conflict & Terrorism*, 28, 413–419,

Nussio, E. (2017). The role of sensation seeking in Violent Armed Group participation. *Terrorism and Political Violence*, 1-19.

Pyszczynski, T., Abdollahi, A., Solomon, S., Greenberg, J., Cohen, F., & Weise, D. (2006). Mortality salience, martyrdom, and military might: The great Satan versus the axis of evil. *Personality and Social Psychology Bulletin*, 32(4), 525–537.

Rice, S. K. (2009). Emotions and terrorism research: A case for a social-psychological agenda. *Journal of Criminal Justice*, 37(3), 248–255.

Rippl, S., & Seipel, C. (1999). Gender differences in right wing extremism: Intergroup validity of a second-order construct. *Social Psychology Quarterly*, 62, 381–393.

Sageman, M. (2004). *Understanding terror networks*. Philadelphia: University of Pennsylvania Press.

Sageman, M. (2008). A strategy for fighting international Islamist terrorists. *The ANNALS of the American Academy of Political and Social Science*, 618(1), 223–231.

Sampson, R. J., & Laub, J. H. (1992). Crime and deviance in the life-course. *Annual Review of Sociology*, 18, 63–84.

Schmid, A. P. (2013). Radicalization, de-radicalization, counter-radicalization: A conceptual discussion and literature review. *ICCT Research Paper*, 97(1), 22. Retrieved from: http://www.icct.nl

Schulten, N., Doosje, B., Spaaij, R., & Kamphuis, J. H. (2019). Psychopathologie en terrorisme: Stand van zaken, lacunes en prioriteiten voor toekomstig onderzoek [Psychopathology and terrorism: State of the art, open questions and priorities for future research]. Amsterdam: Universiteit van Amsterdam.

Silke, A. (1998). Cheshire-cat logic: The recurring theme of terrorist abnormality in psychological research. *Psychology, Crime & Law*, 4, 51–69.

Stephan, W. G., & Stephan, C. W. (2000). An integrated threat theory of prejudice. In: S. Oskamp (Ed.), *Reducing Prejudice and Discrimination* (pp. 23–45). Mahwah, NJ: Lawrence Erlbaum Associates.

Tajfel, H., & Turner, J. C. (1979). An integrative theory of intergroup conflict. *The Social Psychology of Intergroup Relations*, 33(47), 74.

Tripp, B. G. (2007). Fatherhood and Crime: Examining Life Course Transitions Among Men in Harlem. *Doctoral dissertation*, University of Florida.

Van Bergen, D. D., Feddes, A. R., Doosje, B., & Pels, T. V. (2015). Collective identity factors and the attitude toward violence in defense of ethnicity or religion among Muslim youth of Turkish and Moroccan Descent. *International Journal of Intercultural Relations*, 47, 89–100.

Van den Bos, K. (2009). Making sense of life: The existential self-trying to deal with personal uncertainty. *Psychological Inquiry*, 20(4), 197–217.

Van den Bos, K. (2018). *Why people radicalize: How unfairness judgements are used to fuel radical beliefs, extremist behaviors, and terrorism*. Oxford University Press.

Van der Valk, I. & Wagenaar, W. (2010). *Racism & extremism monitor. The extreme right: Entry and Exit*. Amsterdam/Leiden: Anne Frank House/Leiden University.

Van San, M. (2015). Lost souls searching for answers? Belgian and Dutch converts joining the Islamic State. *Perspectives on Terrorism*, 9(5), 47–56.

Venhaus, J. M. (2010). *Looking for a fight: Why youth join Al-Qaida and how to prevent it*. Pennsylvania: U.S. Army War College.

Versteegt, I., Ljujic, V., El Bouk, F., Weerman, F., & van Maanen, F. (2018). *Terrorism, adversity and identity*. Amsterdam: NSCR.

Victoroff, J. (2005). The mind of the terrorist: A review and critique of psychological approaches. *The Journal of Conflict Resolution*, 49, 3–42.

Von Knop, K. (2007). The Female Jihad: Al-Qaida's Women. *Studies in Conflict & Terrorism*, 30, 397–414.

Webber, D., Babush, M., Schori-Eyal, N., Vazeou-Nieuwenhuis, A., Hettiarachchi, M., Bélanger, J. J., ... & Gelfand, M. J. (2018). The road to extremism: Field and experimental evidence that significance loss-induced need for closure fosters radicalization. *Journal of Personality and Social Psychology*, 114(2), 270.

Weenink, A. W. (2015). Behavioral problems and disorders among radicals in police files. *Perspectives on Terrorism*. 9, 17–33.

Weinberg, L., & Eubank, W. L. (1988). Neo-fascist and far left terrorists in Italy: Some biographical observations. *British Journal of Political Science*, 18(4), 531–549.

Wessely, S. (2012). Anders Breivik, the public, and psychiatry. *The Lancet*, 379(9826), 1563–1564.

Willems, H. (1995). Development, patterns and causes of violence against foreigners in Germany: Social and biographical characteristics of perpetrators and the process of escalation. In: T. Bjørgo (Ed.), *Terror from the extreme right*. London: Frank Cass.

Chapter 6

Psychological aspects of radical groups

Goals

- Describe determinants of radicalization at the group level.
- What happens when people join radical groups?
- How are group members being prepared to use violence?
- Summarize and draw conclusions.

Introduction

The 1-million-dollar question is: "What makes a terrorist tick?" or "How can you tell whether a person is about to execute a violent attack?" So far, we have introduced the book (Chapter 1), defined radicalization and terrorism (Chapter 2), discussed methodological concerns (Chapter 3), presented the process of radicalization (Chapter 4), and finally discussed potential background characteristics of radicals (Chapter 5). In this chapter, our aim is to present an overview of the most important processes that occur in radical groups. What do people experience when they join radical groups? In general, these experiences include a strong pressure to think and behave in line with the ideology and behavioral norms of the group. First, new members learn lessons in terms of basic categorization processes, creating strong differences between "us" and "them". Subsequently, we outline common processes that occur in (radical) groups in terms of social influence. Subsequently, we present the group processes that occur during the preparation of a violent attack. Finally, we summarize and draw conclusions in the final section.

As will come clear in this chapter, the questions raised at the beginning are easy to ask but not easy to answer. We argue that even though it is possible to find commonalities in members of radical groups, it is clearly not possible to create a clear profile of "the terrorist" that is 100% bulletproof. Rather, we argue that it is always a unique mix of background factors(Chapter 5), group factors (this chapter), trigger factors in the radicalization process (Chapter 8), and resilience against radical influences (Chapter 7) that ultimately determine whether a person will be able and willing to use violence in order to achieve political and/or societal changes.

Three basic processes in (radical) groups: Categorization, us vs. them, and moral in-group superiority

Humans are social animals. This means that throughout history, humans prefer company for various reasons (Baumeister & Leary, 1995). Among other things, groups can provide people with more safety, with better outcomes (e.g., building a pyramid together) and with better play and more pleasure (e.g., by playing soccer against a rival team) than people can achieve as individuals.

We argue that there are three basic group processes in (radical) groups. First, people are inclined to distinguish between people via a categorization process. By placing people into separate groups (i.e., categorization), it becomes easier to digest all incoming complex social information, because people can use the categories to process and store the information in their memory. In addition, such categorization makes it possible to predict certain traits or behavior of people ("Oh, she is from Denmark, she probably must speak English very well"). Thus, most people use categorizations to make sense and give meaning to the world. This is true for people in radical groups as well.

Second, not only do people place other people into categories – they do that to themselves as well. This creates differentiations between their own group ("us" or the in-group) and other groups ("them" or the out-groups). For example, White inhabitants of Britain may perceive themselves as "British people" and categorize people living in Britain with another skin color as "immigrants" (even when the second generation of these "immigrants" was born in Britain).

Third, this categorization into an in-group and an out-group rarely takes place in a neutral setting. Rather, this in-group versus out-group categorization is almost always associated with different evaluations. Specifically, just as people are inclined to think positively about themselves as individuals in comparison to other individuals, people are also inclined to consider their in-group superior to relevant out-groups (Tajfel & Turner, 1986). For example, White inhabitants of Britain might perceive themselves as superior in norms and values to "immigrants." This perception of in-group superiority may in turn reflect positively on the individual's self-concept (e.g., "I belong to this group that is superior to another group") and consequently result in a relatively high individual self-esteem (based on group membership).

These three basic processes, namely categorization, us versus them, and perceived in-group superiority, are prevalent in most, if not all groups. However, importantly, while we argue that the processes that occur in radical groups are very similar to the processes that occur in other groups, radical groups differ in one aspect from other groups: members of radical groups place a premium on their group membership. In other words, members of radical groups identify strongly with their group and are expected to do so by their group.

This does not so much result in *other* group processes per se. Rather, it results in *stronger* group processes. These stronger group processes occur mainly due to the strong attachment that members feel toward their group. Take the process of categorization. Highly identified Christians, for example, tend to construe their in-group "Christians" in relatively narrow terms and create strong demarcations around their group (Bosveld, Koomen, & Van Der Pligt, 1996). For highly identified Christians, in order for people to be categorized and accepted as real Christians, people have to meet certain strict criteria. These criteria might include that people have to strictly follow certain group rules (e.g., go to church twice on Sunday), display certain ritual behaviors (e.g., pray both before and after each meal – in practice resulting in at least six times a day), obey the rules (often interpreted as laws) as outlined in the Bible, and believe in a literal interpretation of the Bible (e.g., that there is a heaven and a hell that people go to after death). When people do not follow these rules, regulations, and behaviors, they do not meet the criteria, and as such they are not categorized as full in-group members (i.e., true Christians in this case). Of course, people themselves might still consider themselves Christians even if they do not follow all these rules, but for highly identified Christians, these people are not "real" Christians, as these people do not meet the strict criteria that highly identified Christians apply when categorizing people.

This strong need to categorize people is prevalent in all radical groups. All radical groups make clear distinctions between people, especially when it comes to deciding about in-group versus out-group members. People are expected to strongly believe in a certain ideology and to behave strictly in line with this ideology. Almost by definition, there is no room for any moderateness in radical groups, and this is true for the process of categorization as well.

The second group process is making the distinction between us and them. This process is also more strongly prevalent in radical groups. This is apparent in various ways. For example, radical groups often force their members to clearly choose and spend time with their radical group and no longer associate themselves with previous groups (such as family or old friends). Members of radical groups sometimes are forced to stop seeing or texting their parents or old friends in an attempt to create a stronger bond between the comrades, almost replacing the family bond. Second, in the search for highly identified group members, often initiation rituals are performed in radical groups. In most of these rituals, a potential member has to sacrifice something or undergo an unpleasant ceremony. In this manner, the groups wants to see proof that a potential new member is taking the potential new group membership seriously. Third, the us-versus-them process is manifested by the fact that every radical group not only clearly defines an in-group in strict terms, in most ideologies there is also a clear demarcation of a relevant out-group. For example, in Nazi Germany, Jewish people formed a clearly defined out-group whose members differed from the in-group of Aryan people. When at one point the distinction between Jewish and non-Jewish people became not clear enough, Jewish people were forced to wear a star of David to make it clear to everyone that they belonged to this group. Thus, the second group process, making distinctions between us and them, plays a central role in many groups, and this process is even more strongly present in radical groups due to the fact that members of these groups are highly identified.

Finally, the third group process, perceiving the in-group as superior to an out-group, is a common characteristic of many groups. However, this process is central to understanding the dynamics observed in radical groups. All radical groups formulate an ideology in which the in-group is described as superior to an out-group. In some cases, this perceived superiority can be described in tangible things, such as ownership of country: "We were here first, so we have a right to claim this country." In other cases, this perceived superiority can be described in terms of culture or morality: "We are more civilized, because our norms and values are morally superior." Again, in Nazi Germany, this was perhaps most pronounced by the use of the words "Übermenschen" and "Untermenschen" to refer to the Aryan versus non-Aryan people, respectively.

Thus, three basic group processes in terms of (1) categorization, (2) us versus them distinctions, and (3) in-group superiority play a role in almost all groups. For radical groups, however, these processes are all the more important, because members of these groups often identify (or are made to identify) strongly with their group. But how do members of groups influence each other?

Social influence processes

With people being social animals, we do take into account what other people think, say, or do. People have a need to belong to social groups, and the danger of being ostracized from such groups creates a powerful tool to influence people. Parents may punish a child when the child has broken a rule by forcing a moment of cooling down in isolation – meant to make clear that the child needs to change the behavior. In society, when people have broken the law, we separate them from society by putting them in jail – another form of punishment meant to influence future behavior.

As outlined in the previous section, all radical groups provide create a clear categorization and often use strict criteria when evaluating potential new members. This process does not stop when people are accepted into groups. Once people are in groups, social influences can be broken down into two separate processes. On the one hand, there is a process of accentuating intra-group similarities. People are motivated to belong to groups that share common characteristics in order to achieve a common world view and a sense of belonging to a bigger entity or community. The pressure to assimilate into the in-group norm is often very strong in radical and terrorist groups. When people do not follow the in-group norms, they run the risk of being ostracized.

At the same time, the group needs a clearly defined out-group in order to accentuate the differences between the own (superior) group and the other (inferior) out-group. As sometimes group members have to acknowledge that the out-group can be perceived as superior in terms of power (be it military or economical), members of radical groups nearly always perceive the out-group as *morally* inferior. In other words, members of radical groups search for a clearly specified out-group that is depicted as having inferior and unfavorable norms and values. Thus, social influence processes result in an accentuation of both intra-group similarities and intergroup differences (Tajfel & Turner, 1986). Interestingly, this accentuation of intra-group similarities is applied to both the in-group and the out-group. Thus, typically, the out-group is perceived as a unified group with unfavorable characteristics – there are no favorable individual exceptions to the rule.

When applying these notions to radical groups, it is clear that social influence processes play an important role in various phases of the radicalization process. In terms of recruiting new group members (i.e., the transition from a vulnerable to a group membership phase), the social network of an individual is crucial. In his influential work, Sageman (2004) discusses the idea of "a bunch of guys." This claim is supported by the idea that social ties do play an important role, such that there are, for example, brothers (or sisters) who would radicalize together. In addition, there is anecdotal evidence that people from European countries who went to Syria in 2012–2017 to join the Caliphate often knew each other and had lived in the same neighborhood. Similarly, in an empirical study involving 172 Al Qaeda members (from various countries but mostly from Saudi Arabia, Egypt, France, Algeria, Morocco, and Indonesia), Sageman (2001) shows that about 66% of those who joined the Jihad did so collectively with their friends or had a long-time childhood friend already in the Jihad, and another 20% had close relatives already in the Jihad. Thus, the social ties or network of an individual play an important role in radical group membership.

To summarize, in terms of group processes, members of radical groups are encouraged to assimilate into the in-group norms and values. At the same time, the out-group is perceived as a threat to the in-group. This threatening image is combined with an ideology that specifies how the out-group is morally inferior to the in-group and needs to be contained, if necessary by using violence, as we will see in the next section.

Group processes to prepare people for a violent attack

Humans may not be among the most violent animals by nature. Indeed, most people consider it quite a step to start using violence toward other human beings in order to achieve one's goals. This is evident from the fact that people have a tendency to be chicken when it comes to killing another human being. This is particularly the case when the person is in close physical proximity (e.g., Grossman, 1995). Therefore, in order to become an "effective killer," people need to be drilled. How? Group processes can help make people prepared to use violence against an out-group.

A first factor that helps is an ideology. In most ideologies supported by radical groups, there is a clear description of a perceived grievance or perception of injustice (Van den Bos, 2018). For example, the grievance of members of an animal liberation front group is that, in their perception, animals are being treated horribly in the meat and cosmetic industries. In addition, all radical groups argue that their grievance is not well handled by current politicians (or political system as a whole). As this threat from the meat and cosmetic industries is perceived to be eminent, this opens the door to legitimize the use of violence. Thus, an ideology can help to create a situation in which the use of violence is perceived as a viable route of action. In this ideology, perceived out-group threat may strengthen the perceived legitimacy to use violence to defend the in-group: "If we do not act violently now, our enemy will win."

A second factor that makes people more prepared to start using violence is to perceive the out-group not just as a threat, but as a vicious and inhumane enemy. The ultimate manner to describe the viciousness of an out-group is to depict the members of this group as animals and no longer perceive them as humans (Haslam, 2006). This process of dehumanization is a recurring theme not just in radical groups but also in groups involved in warfare. It is an effective way to prepare people for the use violence against other humans. For example, in World War II, Americans sometimes referred to Japanese people as "Japes," a combination of "Japs" and "apes." Better still if one aims to prepare people to use violence against other humans, some groups have used vermin to refer to the out-group (e.g., Hutus referring to Tutsis as "cockroaches" in the 1994 genocide; Nazis referring to Jewish people as "rats" in World War II). This works "better," because these animals are perceived as disgusting and this makes it more logical or even necessary to exterminate this poisonous animal that only spreads diseases.

A third factor to stimulate people's preparedness to use violence is to argue that as the out-group has initiated the violence, the in-group merely is forced to act in self-defense. From this perspective, this out-group needs to be taught a lesson that you cannot fool around with the in-group. At this point, it is important to note that this perceived group threat can start or stimulate an ongoing negative spiral of intergroup behavior. For example, to the extent that an attack on a specific target can result in perceptions of threat, the victimized group may feel the need to defend the in-group by taking revenge on the out-group that has harmed their group in the first attack. In return, the now-victimized group in the revenge action finds itself threatened and considered itself in a legitimate position to "fight back," resulting in a simple and stable pattern of tit-for-tat that often is difficult to reverse. Moghaddam (2018) refers to this as a process of "mutual radicalization" and applies this notion to several historical and current cases of intergroup conflict (e.g., Israel vs. Palestine, China vs. Japan, National Rifle Association vs. gun-regulation groups in the United States).

Thus, while there are others ways of being radical, (some members of) some radical groups choose to use violence to achieve their goals. Some supporters just approve of such violence and may support it either directly (e.g., providing help or shelter for other radicals who use violence) or indirectly (e.g., by providing financial means to prepare and execute a violent attack). Other members of radical groups are motivated, able, and trained to use violence themselves. It helps to believe in a powerful ideology in which the enemy is depicted as threatening and as (disgusting) beasts that can only be eliminated by the use of violence, partly because the out-group is depicted as the first aggressor that the in-group needs to defend itself against.

Summary

In this chapter, we have sketched the most important group processes that influence a process of radicalization. We conclude that in all radical groups, the same processes occur as in other groups, but in a more intense manner: categorizing people, making strong us-versus-them distinctions, and perceiving the in-group as morally superior to out-groups. Members of radical groups influence each other, creating a pressure cooker in which people stimulate a converging world view or ideology. This ideology often consists of one defining theme of grievance, a concern that is really important to them. In the group's perception, the current power holders do not handle this grievance adequately. In addition, an important element of the ideology is that the out-group pose a clear threat to the in-group's main concern. This threat, in combination with a process of dehumanizing the out-group, creates a context in which, in their eyes, the use of violence is both wanted and necessary.

References

Baumeister, R., & Leary, M. R. (1995). The need to belong: Desire for interpersonal attachments as a fundamental human motivation. *Psychological Bulletin*, 117, 497–529.

Bosveld, W., Koomen, W., Van der Pligt, J., & Plaisier, J. W. (1996). Differential construal as an explanation for false consensus and false uniqueness effects. *Journal of Experimental Social Psychology*, 31, 518–532.

Grossman, D. (1995). *On killing: The psychological cost of learning to kill in war and society.* Boston: Little, Brown and Company.

Haslam, N. (2006). Dehumanization: An integrative review. *Personality and Social Psychology Review,* 10, 252–264. http://doi.org/10.1207/s15327957pspr1003_4

Moghaddam, F. M. (2018). *Mutual radicalization: How groups and nations drive each other to extremes.* Washington: APA.

Sageman, M. (2004). *Understanding terror networks.* Philadelphia: University of Pennsylvania Press.

Tajfel, H., & Turner, J. C. (1986). The social identity theory of intergroup conflict. In S. Worchel, & W. G. Austin (Eds), *Psychology of intergroup relations* (pp. 7–24). Chicago: Nelson-Hall.

Van den Bos, K. (2018). *Why people radicalize: How unfairness judgments are used to fuel radical beliefs, extremist behaviors, and terrorism.* New York, NY: Oxford University Press.

Chapter 7

The last straw

Trigger factors in the radicalization process

Goals

- Explains what trigger factors are.
- Provides a review of trigger events at a personal, group, and societal level.
- Draws conclusions about the role of trigger factors in the radicalization process.

Introduction

> Well, I was quite young, 14 or 15-years-old. We went out for a drink in [...].
> I did not really have sentiments to the right, more to the left. Quite leftish.
> It was a mess, there were tensions between [native] Dutch people and immi-
> grants. The tensions rose and every weekend we got into a fight. Then I met
> a friend of my brother. He was a nationalist, red, white and blue [the colours
> of the Dutch national flag]. With that contact it started. I was quite young
> actually.
>
> Excerpt from an interview with a former right-wing extremist
> (Feddes, Mann, & Doosje, 2013)

Many factors are involved in the radicalization process, but what is the straw that breaks the camel's back? The excerpt given previously suggests that meeting a person who is already an extremist was the straw that broke the back of an adolescent boy. The excerpt comes from an interview study we conducted with 3 former right-wing extremists in the Netherlands and 10 former right-wing extremists in Germany (Feddes et al., 2013). Interestingly, all of the persons we interviewed could vividly describe a certain moment or a certain event that "made them" join an extremist group. We call these events *trigger factors*. As can be seen in the Theoretical model on p. ix, trigger factors play a role in all three phases of radicalization. Importantly, trigger factors may also explain why and when individuals move from one phase of radicalization to the next or back. In this chapter, we first examine more in depth what trigger factors are. Subsequently, we provide an overview of trigger factors that have been shown to play a role in the radicalization process based on a literature study we have conducted (Feddes, Nickolson, & Doosje, 2015). We will end the chapter with a summary of the findings and draw some conclusions about the role of trigger factors in the radicalization process.

What are trigger factors?

In the Oxford Dictionary, a trigger is defined as "an event that is the cause of a particular action, process, or situation." In the context of radicalization, we define a trigger factor as *any observable event outside an individual which can lead to further (de) radicalization*. In this sense, trigger factors differ from underlying *psychological needs* of an individual (discussed in Chapter 5) and *root factors* of radicalization (discussed in Chapter 6). Psychological needs (such as the need for identity, justice, significance, or sensation) and root factors (such as relative deprivation or identification with the in-group) are often difficult to measure and observe because they occur in the mind of a person. These needs and root factors are, therefore, hard for policy makers, first-line workers, parents, teachers, and police to anticipate upon. The advantage of trigger factors is that these can be observed and acted upon.

Trigger factors are important, as they may help us understand better when and why individuals move from the *vulnerability phase* to the *group phase* and, ultimately, to the *action phase* (see also the Theoretical model on p. ix). For example, the former right-wing person we interviewed explained that the nationalist person he met introduced him to the right-wing music scene, and there he met other extremists at right-wing music rock concerts, all "big and strong with tattoos, very tough guys" (Feddes et al., 2013). At the same time, his mother was very ill, which caused stress at home. The group provided him with the support he needed: "They were always there for me," he emphasized (Feddes et al., 2013). In terms of psychological needs, this person seems to have had a strong *identity need*: the need to belong to a strong group, a group that provides support. This need may perhaps have been difficult to recognize from the outside, but the events that occurred (meeting a right-wing extremist person, the illness of his mother) were observable and could more easily have been acted upon. Importantly, trigger factors can also lead to *deradicalization*, a notion we discuss further in Chapter 9. In this chapter, we only focus on trigger factors that lead to further radicalization.

In Figure 7.1, the radicalization process is shown for two (fictitious) persons, Person A and Person B. Two different types of trigger factors occur in the radicalization processes of these persons. First, *turning points* are events that introduce a change of direction in the radicalization process. A turning point for the former right-wing extremist we interviewed was meeting the nationalist

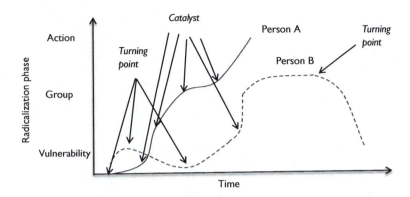

Figure 7.1 Two types of trigger factors (turning points and catalysts) in the (fictitious) radicalization and/or deradicalization process of two individuals.

person who introduced him to the right-wing scene. *Catalysts* are a second type of trigger factors. These are events that accelerate or deaccelerate the radicalization process. For example, an individual may be sensitive to radicalization and merely thinking about joining an extremist group. A *catalyst* can then accelerate this persons' radicalization process, which sets this person on an actual search for a suitable extremist group to join. A catalyst for the former right-wing extremist we talked to may have been a specific fight between native Dutch youth and the immigrant youths, which was the last straw. It may also have been a specific stressful experience at home related to his mother's illness.

Some events may have a stronger impact on a person than other events do. So, what determines the effect of a trigger factor? The *general strain theory* by Robert Agnew (1992) provides us with a starting point in answering this question. In his research, Agnew investigated the question why individuals join criminal groups. To a certain extent, criminal groups are similar to extremist groups (Decker & Pyrooz, 2007; Bovenkerk, 2011; Crone, 2016), and trigger factors seem to play an important role in criminal careers as well (see Box 7.1).

Box 7.1   Trigger factors in extremist groups and criminal groups

Whereas little empirical data are available on radicalization processes (see also Chapter 3 on methods), research on crime provides us with a strong empirical body of work. The link between crime and radicalization has been made by several researchers (Decker & Pyrooz, 2007; Bovenkerk, 2011; Crone, 2016). Despite the fact that there may be differences between criminal groups and extremist groups (e.g., most of the members of criminal groups have a lower socioeconomic background, whereas in terrorist groups, there are also individuals from the middle class and the elite), they do share many similarities. Often, members have a strong group identity reflected in their names. Think of the Islamic extremist group ISIS (Islamic State of Iraq and Syria, also known as Islamic State of Iraq and the Levant) and the right-wing extremist group Blood and Honour. There are numerous examples that can be given of criminal gangs. La Mara Salvatrucha in Los Angeles refers to the ethnic background of its founders (immigrants from El Salvador in the 1950s), with "La Mara" meaning "gang" and "Salvatrucha" being slang for somebody originating from El Salvador. Criminal gangs and extremist groups both have strict norms of loyalty (it is very difficult to step out of the group), and a distinction can be made between leaders and followers. There also are similarities in age in their members, as adolescence is the period when people are most at risk of joining criminal and extremist groups.

What can research on crime teach us about trigger factors? Importantly, some trigger factors that precede crime may also play a role in extremist groups. For example, problems at home, school, or at the workplace as well as bad parenting and divorce (Averdijk, Malti, Eisner, & Ribeaud, 2012; Murray, Farrington, & Sekol, 2012). Other examples are becoming unemployed or dropping out of school (Corner & Gill, 2014). Negative contact with authorities can increase the risk of criminal behavior. In a longitudinal study (which allows for making causal statements; see also Chapter 3 on methods), Ward, Krohn, and Gibson (2014) found that contact with the police *increased* the risk of future violence. This association was particularly strong for low offenders (individuals with a relatively low frequency of crime offenses). Ward and colleagues emphasize that *labeling* may play an important role here. Putting the label "criminal" on a person may actually lead to *more* criminal behavior, a phenomenon psychologists call *self-fulfilling prophecy*. The beliefs others have about a person can influence how a person sees him- or herself and thereby actually make this person behave accordingly.

How about criminals turning to extremism? There are quite a few examples of individuals who make a career change. Crone (2016) points out that 80% of all the perpetrators who committed terrorist attacks in Europe in 2012–2015 had a criminal background. Sixty percent had spent time in prison before committing terrorist acts. Instead of being acquainted with a terrorist ideology that made them turn to violence, it may have been that the violent criminal behavior was *politicized*. This means that an ordinary criminal turns into a politically motivated violent individual. What triggers these individuals to do so? As mentioned later in this chapter, the availability of an extremist group that offers a person with a criminal background an adventurous and meaningful outlook in life may be sufficiently attractive (see also the discussion on psychological needs in Chapter 5). Another example is heroic acts of ingroup members. Perpetrators of the *Charlie Hebdo* attacks in Paris in 2015, the Copenhagen shooting in 2015, and the Berlin truck attack in 2016 all led to praise on Jihadi websites worldwide. Witnessing others go from petty crime to being heroes for a just cause can be a strong trigger factor and, indeed, this theme has been used in propaganda by extremist groups (see Figure 7.2).

Figure 7.2 Propaganda poster used by the British Jihadist group Rayat al-Tawheed in 2014.

The general strain theory poses that people engage in criminal behavior after experiencing stressors over a prolonged period of time. Agnew mentions different stressors such as losing a job and dropping out of school, but also a negative situation at home. Agnew posits that these experiences are stressful to a person and thereby make the person more vulnerable to engaging in criminal behavior. Indeed, research has shown that experiencing multiple stressful life experiences results in more delinquent behavior (Hoffmann & Cerbone, 1999). The general strain theory may help us predict the effect of trigger factors on a person. According to Agnew, the influence of stressors on a person depends on: (1) *strength*: stressors of larger significance have greater impact; (2) *recency*: recent stressors have greater impact than stressors that happened in the past; (3) *duration*: stressors that extend over a longer period of time have greater impact; and (4) *clustering*, when multiple stressors occur simultaneously, this has a stronger impact.

While the general strain theory speaks about stressful experiences over a prolonged period of time, slowly building up the pressure, a trigger factor is the straw that actually breaks the camel's back. We are particularly interested in the question of *which events (or combination of events) can cause a turning point in a person's life or serve as a catalyst*. Why is a certain trigger factor relevant for one person, but not for another person? To answer these questions, we first provide an overview of different trigger factors that have been identified in extremists. We hereby distinguish between (1) trigger factors in the *personal realm*, which refers to events at the *micro level* (Section 7.3); (2) trigger factors that occur in a *group context* (the *meso level*; Section 7.4); and (3) trigger factors in *society* (the *macro level*, Section 7.5). Where applicable, we discuss the specific radicalization stage a trigger factor plays a role in (vulnerability phase, group phase, action phase) and to which psychological need a trigger factor is mostly related (identity need, justice need, significance need, sensation need). We argue that these events have a particularly strong impact on individuals if they are congruent with the dominant psychological need that person has.

Trigger factors in the personal realm

Trigger factors in the personal realm are events that occur in the day-to-day lives of individuals. In this section we review trigger factors that are mentioned in the radicalization literature.

Being confronted with death. This is an often-mentioned trigger factor in the personal realm that plays an important role in the vulnerability phase of radicalization. For example, Mohammed B. (the murderer of filmmaker Theo van Gogh in Amsterdam, the Netherlands, in 2004) said that the death of his mother, who died of breast cancer in 2001, was a turning point in his development. After this moment, he started "a quest for significance" (Buijs, Demant, & Hamdy, 2006, p. 34). Another example is the case of the "Black Widows" (discussed in Chapter 3), wives of Chechen rebels who died in terrorist attacks against Russian targets. The deaths of their husbands "triggered" the wives to turn to violence themselves (Speckhard & Akhmedova, 2006). In a study on suicide terrorism, Lankford (2014) reviewed suicide notes, manifestos, diary entries, internet posts, love letters, martyrdom videos, governmental reports, and other archives. He notes that more than half of the suicide terrorists he examined (66 of the 130) had experienced the unexpected death of a close friend or loved one. In the Netherlands, Van der Valk and Wagenaar (2010) interviewed a former right-wing extremist who stated to have radicalized after the murder of the Dutch filmmaker Theo van Gogh by an Islamic extremist, claiming he wanted to do something against Islamic extremism. In line with this, experimental research on terror management theory (which we also discussed in Chapter 3 on methods) has shown that being confronted with one's own mortality can trigger the radicalization process (Pyszczynski et al., 2006). Students in Iran and the United States were asked to think about their own mortality. They then completed a series of questionnaires asking about their support for (in case of Iranian students) martyrdom attacks against the United States or (in case of U.S. students) support for extreme military interventions that could kill thousands of civilians. Participants who were reminded of death supported the use of extreme violence more.

Negative events at home (domestic problems), losing perspective on work, or *problems at school* can also trigger further radicalization, particularly in the vulnerability phase. For example, a divorce or disagreements with family members can increase an individuals' identity need (social support) or a need for significance (a need for a purpose in life to focus on). Slootman and colleagues (Slootman, Tillie, Majdy, & Buijs, 2009) describe how a radical Muslim man indicated that strong disagreements with his parents about how he lived his life pushed him to focus more strongly on Islam and were an important antecedent of his radicalization process. In a review of life events of 119 terrorists in the United States and Europe, Corner and Gill (2014) found that 20 individuals (17%) had experienced a divorce of their parents. Kleinmann (2012) also points out that problems at home are often important trigger factors for Muslim radicalization. In our interview study with former German right-wing extremists, problems at home were mentioned by three-quarters of the 13 participants (Feddes et al., 2013). One example was the illness of the mother, which was stressful for the former right-wing extremist we mentioned at the start of this chapter. Another former extremist we interviewed explained that his parent's divorce was a trigger in his radicalization process. Besides stressful events at home, stressful events at work or school are also often listed (e.g., Kleinmann, 2012; Lankford, 2012). For example, in a study comparing 81 suicide terrorists and rampage, work, and school shooters in the United States between 1990 and 2010, Lankford (2012) found that three-quarters had experienced problems at school or work.

Concrete and intense experiences with discrimination, racism, and exclusion are considered important trigger factors in the personal realm. Richardson (2012) studied the radicalization process of 41 Americans who travelled to Somalia to join a terrorist group. He argues that experiencing discrimination and exclusion played an important role in their decision to do so. Negative emotions that can result from these experiences, such as hate and contempt, feed into greater support for extreme violent actions (Woodlock & Russell, 2008; Tausch et al., 2011; Feddes, Mann, & Doosje, 2012). *School shooting* incidents provide further evidence supporting the importance of exclusion as a trigger factor. Being excluded was found to be a key factor among 98% of school shooting cases in the United States (McCauley, Moskalenko, & Van Son, 2013).

A confrontation with propaganda is something that often occurs when individuals roam the internet by themselves (but there are examples of propaganda being viewed and discussed in a group context). Extremist groups make use of online communication and social media to instruct potential followers to take matters in their own hands or to join the group. They may also provide material about the ideology or practical information about how to join the group. For example, a study by Bergen (2015) focusing on the radicalization process of 62 jihadists in the United States showed that all individuals were influenced by online propaganda in the vulnerability phase of radicalization. Extremist propaganda often focuses on creating negative emotions in the individual such as hate and contempt by portraying injustice done to the individual or his or her group by referring to discrimination, racism, and exclusion. Propaganda can also match a need for adventure in a person when it portrays romantic images of "warriors on the battlefield" who fight injustice. It can also focus on a need for significance, for example, by stressing that it is possible to leave a criminal past behind and create a "better future," as the propaganda leaflet in Figure 7.2 shows. Note that this poster, used by the British Jihadist group Rayat al-Tawheed in 2014, actually instills a positive emotion in the observer, namely hope.

Meeting a radical person is another trigger factor in the personal realm when an individual is in the vulnerability phase of radicalization and has not yet joined a group. Radicalizing individuals are often motivated by and receive "coaching" from other radical individuals, such as recruiters who instruct their followers with propaganda and the ideology. A charismatic person or individual leader served as a key factor in the radicalization process of several European cases of terrorism, such as Jermaine L., who conducted the 7/7 attack in London in 2005 (Precht, 2007). Former Islamic extremist Maajid Nawaz explains (De Wever, 2015, April 6):

> It was not until a recruiter of Hizb ut-Tahrir approached me that I became enthusiastic. He pointed out the anger that was within me and he offered me a dream. I connected my anger to radical Islam, a deplorable ideology. This step made me a radical.

Often recruiters are charismatic persons who are seen as important because of their position in a group or because they demonstrate knowledge of an ideology or religion. Again, it is important to realize that recruiters, through observation and conversation, identify a person's dominant psychological need (i.e., identity-related needs like safety and a need to belong or justice-related needs) and then "tailor" their approach to this need.

Radical persons that trigger an individual to join a group may be friends or family, but they can also be strangers. Social media such as blogs and online groups are important contexts where individuals are being approached that are difficult to monitor by authorities. An undercover reporter of the Daily Mail posing as a 15-year-old girl in 2015 described how a militant named

"Amatullah" behaved as a "mentor" after the reporter contacted him (Daily Mail, March 8, 2015). The journalist was told that "There's sisters coming every day," a reference to other Muslim women travelling to Syria to join ISIS. The militant gave practical advice about, for example, how and where to buy travel tickets and what type of smartphone to bring. Buijs et al. (2006, p. 28) describe how a member of the Dutch Hofstad Group attempts to convince a 16-year-old boy:

> "You are going agie [brother]. If needed I will pull you into it by your ears. Agie, listen. You are going with me. This is a fact. Start preparing". The boy reacts, "Hey, but this is going too fast for me, I can then not do my [school] exams." The recruiter responds: "Listen, I will tell you one more time. You are going to Pakistan in March to join the Jihad and you are never coming back." The boy hesitatingly admits: "If I think about it now… I feel a bit disgusted [by myself]. I need to get the Jihad spirit in myself again."

Getting married to an extremist is another example of an event in the personal realm that can lead to increased involvement in an extremist group, in particular in the early vulnerability phase of radicalization. A marriage with an extremist can then "pull" a person into an extremist group (see also De Graaf, 2012; Groen & Kranenberg, 2006).

Negative confrontations with authorities and *being detained* are important trigger factors as well. For example, Muslims may experience feelings of unfairness as they feel disproportionally targeted by authorities (Blackwood, Hopkins, & Reicher, 2013). This can give rise to negative emotions such as frustration, hate, and contempt, which, as argued previously, have been shown to play an important role in the process of radicalization. Even though little research exists that conclusively shows that negative confrontations with authorities actually result in radicalization, work in the field of criminology provides some support that it may. In a large longitudinal study (the Rochester Youth Development Study), Ward et al. (2014) could show that contact with the police in adolescence predicts more offending at a later age. This was explained by the fact that *labeling* individuals can strongly influence subsequent behavior (see also Atchison & Heide, 2011). In other words, labeling a person as "radical" may actually serve as a *catalyst* by strengthening the radicalization process over time. Also, being arrested or detained can further strengthen a person's negative image of authorities as being unjust (see also Weggemans & De Graaf, 2015). A former right-wing extremist told Van der Valk and Wagenaar (2010) that being detained created a feeling of being the victim of a conspiracy between Jews and the Dutch state that strengthened his ideology and made him radicalize further.

Besides trigger factors in the personal realm, there are also trigger factors in the context of the group (or meso level), as discussed in the next section.

Trigger factors in the context of groups

The decision to join a group together with peers. As we have already seen in Chapter 6, group processes play an important role in the radicalization process. When individuals actually join an extremist group, a series of group processes make a person radicalize further. Radical groups provide individuals with a feeling of belonging, which is a basic human need (Baumeister & Leary, 1995). Events, rituals, and ceremonies take place in the group context, like organizing demonstrations, learning about the ideology together, and eating together. This results in a greater connectedness to fellow group members and greater identification with the group as a whole. The decision to join the extremist group is a trigger factor that precedes a subsequent series of trigger factors that strongly influence the radicalization process. It is not always the case that individuals decide by themselves to join a group. Groups of like-minded friends can radicalize together and form a new extremist cell (Sageman, 2004). The decision by peers to do so is, therefore, an important trigger factor. This so-called *bunch of guys* phenomenon has also been observed in criminal groups. In a large study involving 1354 youths in the United States, Monahan, Steinberg, and Cauffman (2009) showed that, particularly in the age range of 16 to 20 years, there is a strong influence of peers on development of delinquent behavior. After the age of 20, peer influence was found to be less important.

Breaking social bonds. Once inside, extremist groups often force a person to break outside connections with family and friends who do not share the extremist ideology, a phenomenon that is also called *bridge burning* (Bjørgo & Carlsson, 2005). When radical people break social bonds, they typically radicalize further as the person becomes more resilient against attempts of the outside world to convince them to step out of the group. Recruiters of extremist groups often convince individuals to burn bridges. As a recruiter of the extremist group ISIS put it (Callimachi, 2015, June 27): "We are looking for isolated people. And if they are not yet isolated, we isolate them."

Receiving training is another important trigger factor in the group context. In training, the endurance and motivation of an individual are tested. However, training also serves to indoctrinate the prospective member with an ideology and strengthen social bonds with other group members. Technical and physical activities are important aspects of training, as well as learning and discussing the ideology. Successful training creates a strong *social identity*; the individual starts to identify strongly with the group and the group goals. This is illustrated by the following quote by German radicals who speak about their experiences in training (Bovenkerk & Roex, 2011, p. 146):

> It is a powerful, extremely beautiful and loving brotherhood you share
> with mujahideen [guerilla fighters in Islamic countries who fight against

non-Muslims], brothers from many different countries… Russia, Morocco, Tunisia, Turkey, Europe, Uzbekistan, Tadzhikistan, and Iran. Allah brought all of them together.

Elements of the training can prepare an individual for the *action phase*. For example, to commit individuals to future action, they are asked to make a testament or spoken declaration of intent on a tape recorder or (online) video (Poot & Sonnenschein, 2009). Training can, therefore, serve as a trigger to actually use violence. An example is the case of the Japanese terrorist Kozo Okamoto which was also discussed in Chapter 3. Patricia Steinhof, who interviewed Okamoto, writes (Steinhoff, 1976; p. 837–838):

> Okamoto was impressed both by the training and by the serious commitment to revolution which everybody displayed. He boasted to me that he could now "take on" the Japanese self-defence forces […]. The instruction he did receive was very intense and individualized, however, since there were only four members in his training group. It was not until the seventh and final week of actual military training that Okamoto was told about the Tel Aviv attack plan […]. He was informed that he would participate, and he agreed.

The training in an extremist group can be compared to initiation rituals that are also used in, for example, the armed forces and student fraternities (i.e., hazing rituals; see also Mann, Feddes, Doosje, & Fischer, 2016; Mann, Feddes, Leiser, Doosje, & Fischer, 2017). The ritual is designed to create an intense experience that the group members share with each other. Putting individuals through extreme ordeals, often in isolated places, can make people feel "reborn" and fosters a strong social identity, ultimately creating greater commitment to the group (Whitehouse, 2018). Importantly, training involving tough ordeals or negative emotions (i.e., being humiliated) can also backfire and serve as a turning point in the radicalization process when it does not meet the idealistic and romantic expectations of participants (Bovenkerk & Roex, 2011; Mann et al., 2016, 2017).

Trigger factors in society

Call for action. Trigger factors also occur on a wider societal (macro) level. A call for action is a trigger factor that can motivate individuals who are sensitive to radicalization to join a group or individuals in the group phase to turn to action. An example is the establishment of the Caliphate by ISIS on June 29, 2014, which aimed to encourage Muslims to join the extremist group ISIS. Another example is a call by the spokesman of ISIS, Abu Mohammad al-Adnani, on June

26, 2015, to engage in action. This was followed by terrorist attacks in Tunisia, Kuwait, and France.

A call for action is effective, as it sends a message to the observer that the group is powerful. A strong and powerful group is attractive for people, as it can meet their identity need, the need to counter injustice, the need for significance, or the need for sensation. A call for action creates a concrete and important goal (thereby meeting the need for significance) and may feed into notions of adventure and excitement. The feeling of *not* being able to change injustice done to oneself or the own group is a key factor underlying radicalization (Moghaddam, 2005). A call for action can create the perception that change is feasible and can thereby make people act.

Perceived attack on the ingroup. Another trigger factor at the societal level is a perceived attack on the own group (in-group) such as a military actions, arrests, or cartoons in the media. Framing worldly events as "unjust" is a powerful method to engage radical individuals (Horgan, 2008; Silke, 2008). Extremists often frame their own actions as a response to injustice done to themselves or their own group, such as military interventions by the United States in Islamic counties, which can trigger Islamic extremist violence (Bakker, 2008). The arrest of several RAF-members in the '70s became the symbol for the RAF of a failing West-German law system which, in turn, fed feelings of injustice (Weggemans & De Graaf, 2015). Another well-known example is the hunger strike action by IRA prisoners in the '80s, which became an important symbol for the IRA struggle. Similarly, the cartoons ridiculing the Prophet Mohammad that were published in the Danish newspaper *Politiken* were considered a trigger factor leading to extreme negative emotions among Muslim communities worldwide (Modood, Hansen, Bleich, O'Leary, & Carens, 2006).

Governmental action aimed at the in-group. The last trigger we discuss in this chapter is a governmental action aimed at a particular social group. This is a particularly strong trigger factor when it involves unexpected use of violence, which is perceived by group members as disproportional to their actions (Crenshaw, 1981). The action of the government can induce a spiral of violence as group members' reactions can induce further repressive measures of the government, and so on. Thus, ironically, governmental policies against radicalization can actually trigger *further* radicalization when they are perceived as unjust or out of proportion. An example is the announcement of the Prevent policy by the U.K. government. This policy received the criticism that it focused explicitly on the Muslim community, thereby creating the image that members of the Muslim community were "at risk" of radicalizing and thereby also "risky" (Vermeulen & Bovenkerk, 2012; Heath-Kelly, 2013; Lakhani, 2013). Introduction of policies that are meant to secure societies may, therefore, actually backfire when they result in negative feelings in citizens.

Summary and conclusions

So, what is the straw that breaks the camel's back? In this chapter, we introduced the concept of trigger factors, observable events that make an individual radicalize further, or lead to deradicalization. Furthermore, we identified some trigger factors in the radicalization process that often occur at the personal (micro), group (meso), and societal (macro) level.

Important trigger factors in the *personal realm* are: being confronted with death; a negative event at home (domestic problems); losing perspective on work or problems at school; concrete and intense experiences with discrimination, racism, and exclusion; a confrontation with propaganda; meeting a radical person; getting married to an extremist; negative confrontations with authorities; and being detained. On a *group level*, we found the following trigger factors often occurred: joining a group together with peers, breaking social bonds, and receiving training. Finally, at a *societal level*, we found the following trigger factors to be particularly influential: a call for action, a perceived attack on the in-group, and a governmental action aimed at the in-group.

Based on this review, we can conclude that there is no unique single trigger factor that makes people radicalize. But, as illustrated with the excerpt from the interview with a former right-wing extremist at the start of this chapter, people who join extremist groups often do have a vivid recall of an event or situation that served as the last straw. Importantly, these events can be observed, in contrast to root factors and psychological needs, which are situated in the mind.

We also saw that some trigger factors play a particularly important role in different phases of radicalization. For example, a confrontation with death may motivate a person to join an extremist group or move toward action. Trigger factors at a group level are effective at all stages, as individuals move from a vulnerability phase to a group together or because they are being prepared for action in a group context. Identifying the phase of radicalization a person is in will help in determining the possible effect of a trigger factor on this person.

The phase a person is in can determine the effect of a trigger factor. However, as we saw throughout this chapter, many trigger factors can also be related to an underlying dominant psychological need of a person. Trigger factors in the life of a person may be events related to *identity needs* (i.e., meeting a recruiter who offers friendship), *justice needs* (an experience with discrimination to oneself or one's group members), *significance needs* (a confrontation with death), or *sensation needs* (a call for action). The former right-wing extremist we interviewed seemed to have had a strong identity need (safety and friendship). The members of the right-wing extremist group who "pulled him in" turned this to their advantage. They recognized his needs and offered him safety, social support, and friendship.

Observing psychological needs and trigger factors in a radicalizing person's life can, in a similar manner, help parents, educators, first-line workers, and police to counter it.

Recommended reading

Buijs, F. J., Demant, F., & Hamdy, A. (2006). *Strijders van eigen bodem. Radicale en democratische moslims in Nederland* [*Homegrown Warriors: Radical and democratic Muslims in the Netherlands*]. Amsterdam: Amsterdam University Press.

In this book, Frank Buijs and colleagues describe societal factors that influenced the radicalization process of "salafi" Jihadi (young radical Muslims) after a societal trigger factor that shook the Netherlands, the murder of filmmaker Theo van Gogh in November 2004. Trigger factors such as discrimination, exclusion, and peer influence are discussed.

References

Agnew, R. (1992). Foundation for a general strain theory of crime and delinquency. *Criminology*, 30, 47–87.

Atchison, A. J., & Heide, K. M. (2011). Charles Manson and the Family: The application of sociological theories to multiple murder. *International Journal of Offender Therapy and Comparative Criminology*, 55, 771–798.

Averdijk, M., Malti, T., Eisner, M., & Ribeaud, D. (2012). Parental separation and child aggressive and internalizing behavior: An event history calendar analysis. *Child Psychiatry and Human Development*, 43, 184–200.

Bakker, E. (2008). *Polarisatie en radicalisering [Polarization and radicalization]. Strategische Monitor 2012*. The Hague: Instituut Clingendael.

Baumeister, R. F., & Leary, M. R. (1995). The need to belong: desire for interpersonal attachments as a fundamental human motivation. *Psychological Bulletin*, 117, 497–529.

Bergen, P. (2015). *Jihad 2.0: Social Media in the Next Evolution of Terrorist Recruitment.* Testimony before the U.S. Senate Committee on Homeland Security and Governmental Affairs, 7 May, 2015.

Bjørgo, T., & Carlsson, Y. (2005). *Early intervention with violent and racist youth groups*. Oslo: Norwegian Institute of International Affairs.

Blackwood, L., Hopkins, N., & Reicher, S. (2013). I know who I am, but who do they think I am? Muslim perspectives on encounters with airport authorities. *Ethnic and Racial Studies*, 36, 1090–1108.

Bovenkerk, F. (2011). On leaving criminal organizations. *Crime, Law and Social Change*, 55(4), 261–276.

Bovenkerk, F., & Roex, I. (2011). Terroristen in Trainingskampen [Terrorists in Training Camps]. In: F. Bovenkerk (Ed.), *Een Gevoel van Dreiging [A Feeling of Threat]. Criminologische Opstellen*. Amsterdam: Augustus.

Buijs, F. J., Demant, F., & Hamdy, A. (2006). *Strijders van eigen bodem. Radicale en democratische moslims in Nederland [Homegrown Warriors: Radical and democratic Muslims in the Netherlands]*. Amsterdam: Amsterdam University Press.

Callimachi, R. (2015). ISIS and the lonely young American. *The New York Times*. Retrieved from: http://www.nytimes.com.

Crenshaw, M. (1981). The causes of terrorism. *Comparative Politics*, 13, 379–399.

Crone, M. (2016). Radicalization revisited: violence, politics and the skills of the body. *International Affairs*, 92(3), 587–604.

Corner, E., & Gill, P. (2014). A false dichotomy? Mental illness and lone-actor terrorism. *Law and Human Behavior*, 39, 23–34.

Daily Mail (2015). "Make sure you bring lingerie": Creepy ISIS jihadi grooms undercover reporter posing as 15-year-old girl looking for way to Syria. Retrieved from: dailymail. co.uk.

De Graaf, B. A. (2012). *Gevaarlijke vrouwen. Tien militanten vrouwen in het vizier [Dangerous women. A focus on ten militant females]*. Amsterdam: Boom.

De Wever, R. (2015). De strijd tegen extremisme begint met die voor mensenrechten, stelt deze ex-jihadist [The battle against extremism starts with a fight for human rights this former jihadist says]. De Correspondent. Obtained from: http://www. decorrespondent.nl.

Decker, S. H., & Pyrooz, D. C. (2007). "I'm down for a Jihad": How 100 years of gang research can inform the study of terrorism, radicalization and extremism. *Perspectives on Terrorism*, 9, 104–112.

Feddes, A. R., Mann, L., & Doosje, B. (2012). From extreme emotions to extreme actions: Explaining nonnormative collective action and reconciliation. *Behavioural and Brain Sciences*, 35, 253–268.

Feddes, A. R., Mann, L., & Doosje, B. (2013). *Scientific approach to formulate indicators and responses to radicalisation: Empirical study*. Amsterdam: University of Amsterdam.

Feddes, A. R., Nickolson, L., & Doosje, B. (2015). *Triggerfactoren in het radicaliseringsproces [Trigger factors in the radicalization process]*. The Hague/Amsterdam: Expertise-unit Sociale Stabiliteit/University of Amsterdam.

Groen, J., & Kranenberg, A. (2006). *Strijdsters van Allah. Radicale moslima's en het Hofstadnetwerk [Allah's warriors. Radical female Muslims and the Hofstadgroup]*. Amsterdam: Meulenhoff.

Heath-Kelly, C. (2013). Counter-terrorism and the counterfactual: Producing the "radicalization" discourse and the UK PREVENT strategy. *The British Journal of Politics and International Relations*, 15(3), 394–415.

Hoffmann, J. P., & Cerbone, F. G. (1999). Stressful life events and delinquency escalation in early adolescence. *Criminology*, 37(2), 343–374.

Horgan, J. (2008). From profiles to pathways and roots to routes: Perspectives from psychology on radicalization into terrorism. *The ANNALS of the American Academy of Political and Social Science*, 618, 80–94.

Kleinmann, S. M. (2012). Radicalization of homegrown Sunni militants in the United States: Comparing converts and nonconverts. *Studies in Conflict and Terrorism*, 35, 278–297.

Lakhani, S. (2013). *Radicalisation as a moral career.* Doctoral dissertation, School of Social Sciences, Cardiff University.

Lankford, A. (2012). A comparative analysis of suicide terrorists and rampage, workplace, and school shooters in the United States from 1990 to 2010. *Homicide Studies,* 17, 255–274.

Lankford, A. (2014). Précis of the myth of martyrdom: What really drives suicide bombers, rampage shooters, and other self-destructive killers. *Behavioral and Brain Sciences,* 37, 351–393.

Mann, L., Feddes, A. R., Doosje, B., & Fischer, A. H. (2016). Withdraw or affiliate? The role of humiliation during initiation rituals. *Cognition and Emotion,* 30(1), 80–100.

Mann, L., Feddes, A. R., Leiser, A., Doosje, B., & Fischer, A. H. (2017). When is Humiliation More Intense? The Role of Audience Laughter and Threats to the Self. *Frontiers in Psychology,* 8, 495.

McCauley, C., Moskalenko, S., & Van Son, B. (2013). Characteristics of lone-wolf violent offenders: A comparison of assassins and school attackers. *Perspectives on Terrorism,* 7, 4–24.

Modood, T., Hansen, R., Bleich, E., O'Leary, B., & Carens, J. H. (2006). The Danish cartoon affair: Free speech, racism, Islamism, and integration. *International Migration,* 44, 3–62.

Moghaddam, F. M. (2005). The staircase to terrorism: A psychological exploration. *American Psychologist,* 60, 161–170.

Monahan, K. C., Steinberg, L., & Cauffman, E. (2009). Affiliation with antisocial peers, susceptibility to peer influence, and antisocial behavior during the transition to adulthood. *Developmental Psychology,* 45, 1520.

Murray, J., Farrington, D. P., & Sekol, I. (2012). Children's antisocial behavior, mental health, drug use, and educational performance after parental incarceration: A systematic review and meta-analysis. *Psychological Bulletin,* 138, 175.

Poot, C. J., & Sonnenschein, A. (2009). *Jihadistisch terrorisme in Nederland. Een beschrijving op basis van afgesloten opsporingsonderzoeken [Jihadist terrorism in the Netherlands. A review based on criminal investigation reports]. Wetenschappelijk Onderzoek- enDocumentatiecentrum. Ministerie van Justitie.* Meppel: Boom Juridische Uitgevers.

Precht, T. (2007). *Home grown terrorism and Islamist radicalisation in Europe. From conversion to terrorism.* Danish Ministry of Justice.

Pyszczynski, T., Abdollahi, A., Solomon, S., Greenberg, J., Cohen, F., & Weise, D. (2006). Mortality salience, martyrdom, and military might: The great Satan versus the axis of evil. *Personality and Social Psychology Bulletin,* 32, 525–537.

Silke, A. (2008). Holy warriors exploring the psychological processes of Jihadi radicalization. *European Journal of Criminology,* 5, 99–123.

Slootman, M., Tillie, J., Majdy, A., & Buijs, F. (2009). *Salafi-jihadi's in Amsterdam. FORUM: Reeks Religie en Samenleving.* Amsterdam: Uitgeverij Aksant.

Speckhard, A., & Akhmedova, K. (2006). The new Chechen jihad: Militant Wahhabism as a radical movement and a source of suicide terrorism in post-war Chechen society. *Democracy and Security,* 2(1), 103–155.

Steinhoff, P. G. (1976). Portrait of a terrorist: An interview with Kozo Okamoto. *Asian Survey*, 16(9), 830–845.

Richardson, M. W. (2012). *Al-Shabaab's American recruits: a comparative analysis of two radicalization pathways*. Doctoral dissertation. University of Texas at El Paso.

Sageman, M. (2004). *Understanding terror networks*. Philadelphia: University of Pennsylvania Press.

Tausch, N., Becker, J. C., Spears, R., Christ, O., Saab, R., Singh, P., & Siddiqui, R. N. (2011). Explaining radical group behavior: Developing emotion and efficacy routes to normative and nonnormative collective action. *Journal of Personality and Social Psychology*, 101, 129.

Van der Valk, I. & Wagenaar, W. (2010). *Racism & extremism monitor. The extreme right: Entry and exit*. Amsterdam/Leiden: Anne Frank House/Leiden University.

Vermeulen, F., & Bovenkerk, F. (2012). *Engaging with violent Islamic extremism: Local policies in Western European cities*. The Hague: Eleven International Publishers.

Ward, J. T., Krohn, M. D., & Gibson, C. L. (2014). The effects of police contact on trajectories of violence: A group-based, propensity score matching analysis. *Journal of Interpersonal Violence*, 29, 440–475.

Weggemans, D. & De Graaf, B. A. (2015). *Na de vrijlating: Een exploratieve studie naar recidive en re-integratie van jihadistische ex-gedetineerden [After being released: An explorative study on recidivism and reintegration of jihadist ex-convicts]*. Politie & Wetenschap, Apeldoorn, Universiteit Leiden, Universiteit Utrecht.

Whitehouse, H. (2018). Dying for the group: Towards a general theory of extreme self-sacrifice. *Behavioral and Brain Sciences*, 41, 1–62.

Woodlock, R., & Russell, Z. (2008). Perceptions of Extremism among Muslims in Australia. *Radicalisation Crossing Borders: New Directions in Islamist and Jihadist Political, Intellectual and Theological Thought and Practice Conference*, Melbourne, Vic.

Chapter 8

Resilience against radicalization and deradicalization

Introduction

You become a right-wing extremist if you get beaten up every day and see those images on TV. If that is also reinforced by your group of friends, then I understand that you will, especially if you are young. Then you really start to believe in it and then you feel stronger because you feel good and because you have a goal, you know. So then I understand that you become extremist or radical. But if you grow up in a normal environment where people talk honestly to each other and where parents have good control over you, you will never be radical or extremist, I am convinced of that. If you get a decent upbringing from your parents and are just open in life, you will never become radical. (Respondent K [unassociated], in Bos van den, Loseman, & Doosje, 2009, p. 89).

Why do people turn toward a radical ideology or even choose to become involved in a radical group? As explained in Chapters 5 and 6, joining a radical group can be very attractive to some people. A radical group can offer feelings of connectedness and brother- or sisterhood, a sense of meaning in life, an important goal to strive for, simple answers to difficult questions, and, sometimes, the promise of heroism and paradise after death. People who are vulnerable for different reasons (e.g., the death of a close family member, experienced unfairness, discrimination, humiliation and alienation from society, or a feeling of meaninglessness or disconnectedness [e.g., Moghaddam, 2005; Kruglanski et al., 2013; Doosje et al., 2016]) may therefore more easily be lured into such groups by means of the messages that they convey or they may actively search for radical groups. Still, only a small percentage of people actually join a radical group, and even fewer become actual terrorists. In line with this, remember from Chapter 1 that, strictly in terms of numbers of casualties, terrorism is *not* that important. The amount of deadly victims resulting from traffic accidents, for example, is in that sense a much larger problem for societies.[1] This leads to an important question: Why do radical groups such as IS, Combat18, or AFA (Anti Fascist Action, a Dutch Flemish extreme-left network) actually fail to recruit more people who are willing and able to commit violence or to support others who commit violence? There are many vulnerable young people all over the world who experience psychological difficulties but who *do not* radicalize. Why is this the case? Why do not all these people become terrorists? One of the answers to this question is: because they are *resilient* to the extremist messages of these groups.

Resilience, very generally described as the ability to recover or "bounce back" after change or misfortune (Resilience, n.d.), is, as we shall see, a concept that is used in many different fields and in many different ways. But what is resilience in the context of (de)radicalization, exactly? How can it be defined? And which factors determine or predict whether someone (or a group) is resilient to extreme ideas? In the current chapter, we will define and discuss *resilience against extremist messages*, and we will devote particular attention to the factors that predict this type of resilience, so-called *protective factors*.

This chapter is structured as follows: First, we will briefly introduce the general concept of resilience as used in many fields ranging from ecology to psychiatry. Building on this, we discuss resilience in the context of radicalization, mainly in terms of resilience against extremist messages, and explain how this can be predicted by the way an individual thinks, feels, and behaves. We will also explain how, in the later stages of radicalization, people can become resilient against *de*radicalization. In other words, how the so-called "shield of resilience" can turn around and prevent radical individuals from leaving their ideology and group behind. We will end the chapter with a brief summary of the research and theories discussed and draw conclusions.

What is resilience?

Origin of the term and general definition

The term "resilience" stems from the Latin word *resilio*, which means "to jump back" (Manyena, 2006). Although the concept only recently gained popularity in radicalization studies, it has a longer history in disciplines such as ecology, economy, physics, and engineering, and also in medicine, psychology, and psychiatry (e.g., Bonanno, 2004; Gallopín, 2006; and see Manyena, 2006; Earvolino-Ramirez, 2007; Norris, Stevens, Pfefferbaum, Wyche, & Pfefferbaum, 2008; Mohaupt, 2009). In the more technical fields, resilience refers to "the capacity of a material or system to return to equilibrium after a displacement" (Norris et al., 2008, p. 127). In other words, the resilient system is a system that is flexible, adaptable, and able to withstand external forces by "bouncing back" and returning to its original state.

This idea is used in a psychological sense in clinical psychology and psychiatry, where it is mainly studied in relation to trauma, loss, and stress (e.g., Bonanno, 2004; Rutter, 2006; Neff & Broady, 2011). In this context, resilience reflects an ability of people to successfully cope with such events. In the clinical field, resilience is therefore defined as: "an interactive concept that refers to a relative resistance to environmental risk experiences, or the overcoming of stress or adversity" (Rutter, 2006, p. 1). Several factors have been identified that can help in this coping process. These are called "protective factors": specific competencies, attributes, or situations needed for resilience to occur (e.g., Dyer & Minton McGuinness, 1996; Earvolino-Ramirez, 2007, p. 75). Such factors, such as self-confidence, a broad social network, flexibility, and trust, are good predictors of how resilient an individual is (e.g., Rutter, 1987). The clinical literature describes many of these factors, both on a *cognitive* (thinking) level, an *emotional/motivational* (feeling) level, and a *behavioral* (acting) level. These general factors are also relevant for resilience to radicalization, and we will discuss them extensively later in this chapter. First, we introduce the concept of resilience in the context of (de)radicalization and present our own definition of this type of resilience.

Resilience in the context of (de)radicalization

In government circles and academia, the idea of resilience against radicalization has gained much popularity over time, and the term "resilience" has now become a real *buzzword* among politicians and scholars. In many countries all over the world, strengthening the (psychological) resilience of individuals as well as communities is considered a key tool in the fight against extremism. For example, the Canadian report "Building Resilience against Terrorism. Canada's Counter-Terrorism Strategy" states: "Resilience is both a principle and an underlying theme of the Strategy. Building a resilient Canada involves fostering a society in which individuals and communities are able to withstand violent extremist ideologies and challenge those who espouse them" (Government of Canada, 2013, p. 11). Likewise, a report by the European Commission states that: "Over the last decade, the European Commission has invested heavily in combating this threat [of violent extremism] by addressing conditions conducive to violent extremism, building capacity to reinforce the rule of law, promote development and strengthen the resilience of vulnerable communities" (European Commission, 2019, p. 5).

Thus, resilience plays an important, even key, role in these programs. However, in these and other reports, resilience in the specific context of radicalization is not clearly defined and seems to involve different meanings on different levels of analysis: individual (micro), group (meso), and community (macro). For example, in a letter written by the Dutch Ministry of Security and Justice about the integrated approach to terrorism (Grapperhaus, 2017), one of the goals mentioned is "the strengthening of digital resilience and tackling extremism online" (p. 2). However, it is unclear what is meant by this type of resilience and how it can be strengthened.[2] As another example, the report by the European Commission mentioned previously indicates the following about the concept of resilience: "'Resilience' is a contentious and complex term but refers here to a wide range of factors (ideas, institutions, trends and values) that enable individuals and/or communities to resist, or recover from, the specific contributory dynamics feeding violent extremism" (p. 13). Hence, although resilience is defined in this report, the concept remains very broad and vague.

Although terrorism is complex and dynamic, and therefore resilience in the context of (counter)terrorism can take many different forms (Dechesne, 2016, p. 415), keeping the concept this broad and vague may reduce an interesting and useful construct to a very general, even hollow concept that cannot easily be measured. In the current chapter, we therefore focus on one specific type of resilience in the context of (de)radicalization. We clearly delineate the elements it is predicted by and the role it can play in the different phases in the process of radicalization, while acknowledging the relevance of other types of resilience (see Box 8.1). Before we dive deeper into conceptualizing resilience, consider the following quote by Celal Altuntas, a Dutch former PKK (the Kurdistan Workers Party, which is a far-left militant organization) combatant.

> I disapprove, and yet understand their [vulnerable, insecure and socially marginalized young people's] powerlessness. I experienced that powerlessness myself. It took a long time before I could really distance myself from various forms of radicalism. My parents gave me love and warmth and they kept talking to me. Partly because of that, I dared to be vulnerable, in my cultural inner world and in the western outer world (Altuntas, 2014).

This example shows the type of resilience that we focus on in this chapter. Altuntas experienced some inner struggles and insecurities. However, because his parents supported him, showed him love and warmth, and kept talking to him, he could, with their help, work on these problems and did not need extremist groups to channel his feelings. This is one example of how people can become resilient against extreme ideologies. In terms of the process of radicalization (see Theoretical model on p. ix), this type of resilience is situated in the vulnerability phase or in early stages of the group phase but is not very likely to be present when people have become more involved in the extremist group (when they are heading toward the action phase). This is because these phases are characterized by strong adherence to extreme ideas, black-and-white concepts of the world, and bridge burning (see Chapter 4).

So how to define this type of resilience and how to distinguish it from other types of resilience? There are different types of resilience that are situated at different levels (micro, meso, macro) and with different actors playing a key role. For example, Dechesne (2016) describes five types of resilience in the context of counterterrorism (see Box 8.1). Most relevant for the current chapter is his definition of *ideological resilience:* "the ability of potential supporters of the violent opposition to withstand the ideology [i.e., extremist ideas] of the violent opposition" (p. 419). Our own conceptualization of resilience builds further on this definition. Based on our previous research (Mann et al., 2015), we define resilience against extremist messages as "the extent to which individuals withstand and/or resist or oppose extremist influences on the basis of cognitive, emotional, and behavioral protective factors" (see Mann et al., 2015, p. 28).

Thus, this definition of resilience is in line with Dechesne's (2016) description of ideological resilience, as it highlights the aspect of *resistance.* At the same time, it is more elaborated, as we consider different cognitive, emotional, and behavioral protective factors and take into account the *process* of radicalization. That is, this definition reflects the early phase of radicalization, but resilience has a different meaning at different points in the process; for example, it can "turn around" at a certain point (see Section "Resilience against deradicalization"). As this happens, different protective factors may become relevant. Importantly, this definition of resilience applies to the individual, that is, the micro level of analysis. As mentioned previously (and see Box 8.1), resilience can also be applied to groups (meso) and societies or governments (macro). However, this book is primarily concerned with the radicalization – and therefore resilience – of the individual.

Box 8.1   Types of resilience in the context of counterterrorism

Dechesne (2016, p. 419) defines five different types of resilience in the context of counterterrorism:

Psychological resilience refers to "a psychological capacity to maintain equanimity in the presence of a real threat and the ability to bounce back after being exposed to terror-induced trauma." Thus, this type of resilience concerns the people under threat of terrorism or the victims of a terrorist attack. This form of resilience can be extended to the group level. *Community resilience* is therefore described as "the ability of a society/community to maintain cohesion under the threat of terrorism and to recover from terrorist attacks."

Resilience can refer to different types of actors: potential victims of terrorism, or potential perpetrators. *Ideological resilience* refers to the potential perpetrators (individual or group) and is defined as "the ability of potential supporters of the violent opposition to withstand the ideology [i.e., extremist ideas] of the violent opposition." Dechesne (p. 419) also considers the ability to "recover from extremist thought once it has become a significant part of the life of an individual or a community" part of this type of resilience.

Next, *political resilience* refers to the "political ability of governing and opposing political parties to take a unified stance against violence while disagreeing over other, high-stakes issues." Finally, *international resilience* refers to "[the] ability of the government and country to maintain its international reputation while involved in counterterrorism efforts."

Importantly, as we can infer from these different types of resilience, we need to take into account the *different levels* on which resilience is relevant. Resilience on the individual (micro) level, resilience on the group (meso) level, and resilience on the societal (macro) level. For example, psychological resilience, as described previously, refers to the micro level, whereas community resilience refers to the meso level. Ideological resilience may refer to a radicalizing individual as well as a radicalizing group, so it can be both micro and meso level. Finally, political and international resilience refer to the macro level.

Additionally, as indicated previously, resilience can refer to *different types of actors*, depending on whether one considers the potential *victims* of terrorism or the potential *perpetrators/supporters* of terrorism. Psychological resilience concerns the people under threat of terrorism or the victims of a terrorist attack, whereas ideological resilience refers to the (potentially) radicalizing individual or group who may become (a) terrorist(s) or support terrorist acts.

Thinking, feeling, and behaving: Predictive factors of resilience against radicalization

Now that we have a definition of resilience, the question is: What actually makes an individual resilient against radicalization? As discussed previously, resilience in the clinical context refers to a kind of coping strategy, and certain cognitive, emotional, and behavioral protective factors can predict how resilient an individual is. Interestingly, we can identify similar protective factors that could predict resilience against radical messages (Mann et al., 2015). We discuss these factors below.

Cognitive protective factors. Cognition is the overarching term used to describe how people *think*. This concerns, for example, how people perceive events, how they process information, and how they retrieve information from memory. In the clinical domain, cognitive protective factors thus deal with how people perceive, process, and retrieve information related to trauma, stress, or adversity. Such factors include flexibility and the ability to "bounce back" or reintegrate after adversity or change. This is, in turn, related to a complex and self-reflective cognitive style: the ability to reflect on the self and on the way one deals with stressors or change in one's life. In addition, an active and effective coping style and the ability to reinterpret and reappraise experiences, that is, looking at a situation in a different way and taking a different perspective, are considered important protective factors (e.g., Bonanno, 2004; Rutter, 2006; Earvolino-Ramirez, 2007).

The way people think is also likely to play an important role in resilience in the context of radicalization. How people perceive and cognitively process events in their personal lives, in their social groups, and in society at large predicts in part how they feel about these things and how they (would like to) act. Previously, we mentioned that (clinically) resilient people have a *complex and self-reflective cognitive style*. A cognitive-motivational concept that is relevant in this regard is the need of an individual for *cognitive closure*, that is "a desire for definite knowledge on some issue" (Kruglanski & Webster, 1996, p. 263). People who have a strong need for cognitive closure prefer situations that are clear and unambiguous, and they try to avoid ambivalence. They are thus more likely to interpret situations and issues in a black-and-white manner rather than acknowledging and accepting that there are several different perspectives on some issue and there is not always "right" and "wrong." Thus, these people do not have a very complex and self-reflective cognitive style. In addition, research shows that the need for cognitive closure can enhance in-group identification and out-group derogation (Orehek et al., 2010), which likely enhances the in-group–out-group dichotomy (thinking in terms of "us" and "them") and may be caused by this as well. On the other hand, when an individual's need for cognitive closure is low, this allows for a more complex way of thinking, which makes them more open to different opinions and different interpretations of the same situation and prevents a black-and-white interpretation of the world.

Importantly, this is exactly the opposite of what extremist groups strive for. Extremist groups are characterized by their closed-mindedness, a need for clear and definite answers to complex questions, and a rejection of different values and viewpoints (see Chapter 6). Such groups are therefore more attractive to people with a high need for cognitive closure. Furthermore, once people are part of an extremist group, a strong need for cognitive closure can contribute to compliance with the group consensus, which may lead to a stronger endorsement of the group goals (Kruglanski et al., 2014). We thus may consider individuals with a strong need for cognitive closure less resilient to extremist ideas and propaganda, whereas people who have a low need for closure can be considered more resilient to extremism.

Emotional protective factors. These factors relate to how people *feel* about themselves and others and about events that are relevant for the self. In the clinical resilience literature, feelings of (self-)confidence, personal agency, self-determination, self-efficacy (the belief that one has influence over their circumstances and the outcome of events), and self-enhancement are identified as important protective factors. These feelings are related to a sense of meaning in life: having a meaningful purpose (Mann et al., 2015). In addition, a feeling of connectedness to others and the community is an important protective factor (e.g., Dyer & Minton McGuinness, 1996; Bonanno, 2004; Rutter, 2006). As with the cognitive factors, these emotional protective factors are also important in the context of radicalization.

First, a sense of meaning in one's life and having a meaningful purpose are relevant when it comes to resilience to radicalization (see Dechesne, 2016). When people feel such meaning is lacking, for example, because they often experience negative emotions such as anger, frustration, or humiliation, or because they experience discrimination, they may be triggered to start a "quest for significance." A quest for significance is defined as "the fundamental desire to matter, to be someone, to have respect" (Kruglanski et al., 2014, p. 73, and see Kruglanski, Chen, Dechesne, Fishman, & Orehek, 2009; Kruglanski et al., 2013). Under certain conditions (i.e., group processes and ideology), this quest may result in people joining a radical group and starting to endorse or use violence to reach this groups' goals. We may thus consider people who experience a sense of meaning and feel they have important goals in life (of course, we refer to goals other than those of a radical group) more resilient against extremist influences, whereas people in whom a quest for significance is activated are less resilient.

As indicated previously, a quest for significance may be activated by experiencing negative emotions, for example, after being humiliated or discriminated. Thus, for people to be more resilient, it is important to be able to cope with and regulate such feelings (see Mann et al., 2015). At the same time, experiencing positive emotions such as hope, trust, self-control, and self-efficacy helps strengthen the shield of resilience (Mann et al., 2015; and see also Tugade, Fredrickson, & Barrett, 2004; Dechesne, 2016). In particular institutional trust, the trust in authorities, such as the government, police, and rule of law, is important in this regard, because the process of radicalization goes hand in hand with a decline of trust in society and in the political system in a society (Slootman & Tillie, 2006). A sense of connection to others and to the community in general (which was also identified as protective factor in the clinical domain) lays the basis for such institutional trust. Social capital theory

(Putnam, 2000) highlights this connection and states that people are more likely to trust institutions if they feel strongly connected to others in their social environment.

Thus, we consider people more resilient to extremist messages if they experience their lives to be meaningful and feel they have an important goal to strive for; feel self-confident; do not experience extreme negative emotions, but if they do, are able to regulate them; and experience many positive emotions such as hope and trust in society, possibly via strong connections with other people and the community in general.

Behavioral protective factors. These factors all have to do with how people *act*. A very important concept in this regard is "social capital." Social capital can be understood as having and maintaining positive relationships with others; being active in different social groups, religious organizations, schools, the neighborhood, or the community; and looking for support when needed. In the clinical literature, these aspects are all associated with more resilience (e.g., Bonanno, 2004; Rutter, 2006; Norris et al., 2008).

Importantly, groups can form a material and psychological buffer against negative experiences and major life events (e.g., migration, disease, death of a family member), and being part of more groups means having more resources available. Research has shown that being a member of and identifying with multiple diverse groups (i.e., multiple group memberships) positively predicts well-being and resilience in the face of major life events and challenges (Haslam et al., 2008; Iyer, Jetten, Tsivrikos, Postmes, & Haslam, 2009; Jones & Jetten, 2011). Other research shows that being a member of multiple groups (e.g., work teams, school classes, study groups, hobby clubs, religious groups, volunteer groups, etc.) boosts self-esteem because these groups are a source of pride and give meaning to people's lives (Jetten et al., 2015).

These factors are similarly relevant for resilience against radicalization. As we discussed in the section on emotional protective factors, a feeling of connectedness to others and society is an important basis for trust and makes people more resilient to radicalization. When people act upon these feelings of connectedness and trust and when they act in ways that promote such feelings, they can, therefore, be considered more resilient as well. When they are a member of and identify with multiple different groups, they also come into contact with more diverse opinions, ideas, and values. This may help to prevent a "narrowing" of thought, which can make people less vulnerable to the black-and-white messages of extremist groups (see Mann et al., 2015). Note that the promotion of diverse opinions, ideas, and values via different social groups is related to the cognitive protective factors described previously. Importantly, in line with the idea that multiple group memberships make people more resilient to radicalization, Bhui, Everitt, and Jones (2014) found that resilience against radicalization among Muslims in East

London and Bradford, which they measured as "condemnation of violent protest and terrorism," is associated with a larger number of social contacts.[3]

As indicated previously, by means of bridge burning (a trigger; see Chapter 7), radical groups try to cut off all contacts other than the ones with the in-group to create tunnel vision. According to McCauley and Moskalenko (2008): "Groups differ in their power to set moral standards. The social reality value of a group is weak to the extent that members belong to other groups with competing standards of value. Conversely, the social reality value of a group is strong when members are cut off from other groups" (p. 423). Thus, people who have many positive social relations; look for support when needed; and belong to, are active in, and identify with multiple diverse groups are more resilient to extremist messages.

Importantly, some of the factors that promote resilience against radicalization seem to be the same factors that make people less vulnerable to radicalization (see Chapters 4 and 6). Could we therefore conclude that resilience and vulnerability are opposites? The answer to this question is no. Although, in general, resilience and vulnerability are probably negatively related to each other, in the sense that more vulnerability is associated with less resilience and vice versa, we should consider them two different concepts (e.g., Manyena, 2006; Toma, 2014). That is, resilience does not necessarily mean the absence of vulnerability (Waller, 2001). For example, people can be vulnerable to radical ideas in some respects, but at the same time, they can possess a certain level of resilience to those influences. Vulnerability and resilience can also be predicted by different protective factors. For example, an individual may be emotionally vulnerable but might possess cognitive capacities that make him or her resistant. We should therefore consider resilience and vulnerability negatively related, yet separate concepts (Mann et al., 2015, p. 29–30).

Resilience against deradicalization

Until now, we have mostly discussed how people can become resilient against extreme ideas and messages, assuming that these people do not have extremist ideas yet or that these ideas are not fully developed but that people may be vulnerable to such ideas. Thus, this concerns people in the vulnerability phase and the beginning of the group phase of radicalization. However, some people are already radicalized to some extent, are part of an extremist group, or are even on the verge of committing or actively supporting the execution of a violent act. Thus, these people are approaching (or are already in) the action phase of the process of radicalization. We can assume that such people are not resilient to radicalization (anymore) because they have already been radicalized to a large degree. It is more likely that these people are immune to criticism of the radical group or counter-narratives, if they are exposed to them at all (see Van Eerten, Doosje, Konijn, de Graaf, & de Goede 2017).

This would imply that at a certain point in the process of radicalization, an individuals' potential resilience against radicalization turns into resilience against deradicalization. That is, the protective "shield of resilience" turns around and prevents deradicalization (Doosje et al., 2016, and see our Theoretical model on p. ix). When exactly this turning point takes place may differ per person, and how quickly or slowly this happens (is it a turning point or a turning phase?) may also differ. A key process here is the "bridge burning" (Bjørgo & Carlsson, 2005) we already mentioned previously. The more people cut off contacts with former friends, family, and other people and groups in their lives, the less likely it is that they will come across different opinions and have the opportunity to take a different perspective or consider viewpoints different from the one the radical group propagates. We consider it likely that precisely when this happens, people develop strong resilience against deradicalization, which is, of course, also the reason radical groups consider bridge burning so important in the process. In Chapter 9 on deradicalization, we will discuss this process as well and explain what happens if the shield of resilience against deradicalization falls apart.

Summary

In this chapter, we discussed resilience against extremist messages, which we define as: "the extent to which individuals withstand and/or resist or oppose extremist influences on the basis of cognitive, emotional, and behavioral protective factors." We explained how this type of resilience can be predicted by the way people think, feel, and behave. For example, an individual who has an open worldview and does not have a strong need for cognitive closure, feels confident and in control over his/ her life, experiences meaning in life, and has a large and various social network in which he or she is active can be considered more resilient to extremist messages. Importantly, at a certain point in the process of radicalization, the shield of resilience can turn around, and the individual becomes resilient to deradicalization. With the current chapter, we tried to offer more insight into one specific type of resilience against radicalism. More clarity about this concept in this field of radicalization and consensus about its meaning can help in building evidence-based practical tools and interventions to stimulate resilience against radicalization, thereby preventing radicalization and promoting deradicalization (see also Chapter 9).

Endnotes

1. In Chapter 1, we also indicate that terrorism has important psychological consequences, and of course we do not wish to downplay these consequences here. At the same time, we would like to put into perspective the amount of people who actually become terrorists and the amount of attacks they commit.

2. In the accompanying note, this is also not further explained. See: https://www.nctv.nl/binaries/TK%20Bijlage%20Integrale%20aanpak%20terrorisme_tcm31-290983.pdf. Note that this document is written in Dutch.

3. They also found that resilience was related to *less* social capital (measured as satisfaction with the neighborhood, trust in neighbors, and feelings of safety). However, in this study, low social capital means less satisfaction with the neighborhood, less confidence, and more fear. Thus, the people who report low social capital may therefore also be more afraid of terrorist attacks. It makes sense that exactly these people reject terrorist violence more strongly.

Recommended reading

Dechesne, M. (2016). "The concept of resilience in the context of counterterrorism." In: U. Kumar (Ed.), *The Routledge International Handbook of Psychosocial Resilience*. Oxford, UK: Routledge.

This chapter presents a useful overview of different types of resilience in the context of radicalization and deradicalization.

References

Altuntas, C. (2014, October 18). *Ik was zo'n radicale jongen waar IS op loert [I was such a radical boy that IS is lurking for]*. Trouw. Retrieved from https://www.trouw.nl/nieuws/ik-was-zo-n-radicale-jongen-waar-is-op-loert~b6d77371/

Bhui, K., Everitt, B., & Jones, E. (2014). Might depression, psychosocial adversity, and limited social assets explain vulnerability to and resistance against violent radicalisation? *PLOS ONE*, 9(9). doi: 10.1371/journal.pone.0105918.

Bjørgo, T., & Carlsson, Y. (2005). *Early intervention with violent and racist youth groups (NUPI Working Papers, issue 667)*. Oslo: Norwegian Institute of International Affairs. Retrieved via http://www.isn.ethz.ch/Digital-Library/Publications/Detail/?id=27305&lng=en

Bonanno, G. A. (2004). Loss, trauma, and human resilience: Have we underestimated the human capacity to thrive after extremely aversive events? *American Psychologist*, 59, 20–28.

Bos van den, K., Loseman, A., & Doosje, B. (2009). Waarom jongeren radicaliseren en sympathie krijgen voor terrorisme. Onrechtvaardigheid, onzekerheid en bedreigde groepen. WODC rapport, projectnummer: 1626. Retrieved via https://www.wodc.nl/onderzoeksdatabase/jongeren-aan-het-woord-over-radicalisme-en-terrorisme.aspx#project-informatie.

Dechesne, M. (2016). "The concept of resilience in the context of counterterrorism." In: U. Kumar (Ed.), *The Routledge International Handbook of Psychosocial Resilience*. Oxford, UK: Routledge.

Doosje, B., Moghaddam, F. M., Kruglanski, A. W., De Wolf, A., Mann, L., & Feddes, A. R. (2016). Terrorism, radicalization and de-radicalization. *Current Opinion in Psychology*, 11, 79–84.

Dyer, J. G., & Minton McGuinness, T. (1996). Resilience: Analysis of the concept. *Archives of Psychiatric Nursing*, 10, 276–282.

Earvolino-Ramirez, M. (2007). Resilience: A concept analysis. *Nursing Forum*, 42, 73–82.

European Commission. (2019). *STRIVE for development. Strengthening resilience to violence and extremism*. Luxembourg: Publications Office of the European Union. Retrieved from https://ct-morse.eu/strive-for-development-strengthening-resilience-to-violence-and-extremism-2/

Gallopín, G. C. (2006). Linkages between vulnerability, resilience, and adaptive capacity. *Global Environmental Change*, 16, 293–303.

Government of Canada (2013). *Building resilience against terrorism. Canada's counter-terrorism strategy*. Retrieved via http://www.publicsafety.gc.ca/cnt/rsrcs/pblctns/rslnc-gnst-trrrsm/index-eng.aspx

Grapperhaus, F. (2017, November 24). *Aanleidingsbrief integrale aanpak terrorisme [Instruction letter integral approach terrorism]* Ministerie van Justitie en Veiligheid. Retrieved from https://www.rijksoverheid.nl/documenten/kamerstukken/2017/11/24/tk-aanbiedingsbrief-integrale-aanpak-terrorisme

Haslam, C., Holme, A., Haslam, S. A., Iyer, A., Jetten, J., & Williams, W. H. (2008). Maintaining group memberships: Social identity continuity predicts well-being after stroke. *Neuropsychological Rehabilitation*, 18(5–6), 671–691.

Iyer, A., Jetten, J., Tsivrikos, D., Postmes, T., & Haslam, S. A. (2009). The more (and the more compatible) the merrier: Multiple group memberships and identity compatibility as predictors of adjustment after life transitions. *British Journal of Social Psychology*, 48, 707–733.

Jetten, J., Branscombe, N. R., Haslam, S. A., Haslam, C., Cruwys, T., Jones, J. M., ... & Thai, A. (2015). Having a lot of a good thing: Multiple important group memberships as a source of self-esteem. *PLOS ONE*, 10(5), e0124609.

Jones, J. M., & Jetten, J. (2011). Recovering from strain and enduring pain. Multiple group memberships promote resilience in the face of physical challenges. *Social Psychological and Personality Science*, 2, 239–244.

Kruglanski, A. W., Chen, X., Dechesne, M., Fishman, S., & Orehek, E. (2009). Fully committed: Suicide bombers' motivation and the quest for personal significance. *Political Psychology*, 30, 331–357

Kruglanski, A. W., Bélanger, J. J., Gelfand, M., Gunaratna, R., Hettiarachchi, M., Reinares, F., Orehek, E., Sasota, J., & Sharvit, K. (2013). Terrorism - A (self) love story: Redirecting the significance quest can end violence. *American Psychologist*, 68, 559–575.

Kruglanski, A. W., Gelfand, M. J., Bélanger, J. J., Sheveland, A., Hetiarachchi, M., & Gunaratna, R. (2014). The psychology of radicalization and deradicalization: How significance quest impacts violent extremism. *Political Psychology*, 35, 69–93.

Kruglanski, A. W., & Webster, D. M. (1996). Motivated closing of the mind: "Seizing" and "freezing." *Psychological Review*, 103, 263–283.

Mann, L., Doosje, B., Konijn, E. A., Nickolson, L., Moore, U. & Ruigrok, N. (2015). Indicatoren en manifestaties van weerbaarheid van de Nederlandse bevolking tegen extremistische boodschappen (p. 21). WODC.

Manyena, S. B. (2006). The concept of resilience revisited. *Disasters*, 30, 434–450.

McCauley, C., & Moskalenko, S. (2008). Mechanisms of political radicalization: Pathways toward terrorism. *Terrorism and Political Violence*, 20, 415–433.

Moghaddam, F. M. (2005). The staircase to terrorism: A psychological exploration. *American Psychologist*, 60, 161–169.

Mohaupt, S. (2009). Review article: Resilience and social exclusion. *Social Policy and Society*, 8, 63–71.

Neff, L. A., & Broady, E. F. (2011). Stress resilience in early marriage: Can practice make perfect? *Journal of Personality and Social Psychology*, 101, 1050–1067.

Norris, F. H., Stevens, S. P., Pfefferbaum, B., Wyche, K. F., & Pfefferbaum, R. L. (2008). Community resilience as a metaphor, theory, set of capacities, and strategy for disaster readiness. *American Journal of Community Psychology*, 41, 127–150.

Orehek, E., Fishman, S., Dechesne, M., Doosje, B., Kruglanski, A. W., Colee, A. P., Saddler, B., & Jackson, T. (2010). Need for closure and the social response to terrorism. *Basic and Applied Social Psychology*, 32, 279–290.

Putnam, R. (2000). *Bowling alone: The collapse and revival of American community*. New York: Simon & Schuster.

Resilience. (n.d.). In *Merriam-Webster.com dictionary*. Retrieved from https://www.merriam-webster.com/dictionary/resilience#note-1

Rutter, M. (1987). Psychosocial resilience and protective mechanisms. *American Journal of Orthopsychiatry*, 57, 316–331. doi: 10.1111/j.1939-0025.1987.tb03541.x

Rutter, M. (2006). Implications of resilience concepts for scientific understanding. *Annals of the New York Academy of Sciences*, 1094, 1–12.

Slootman, M., & Tillie, J. (2006). *Processen van radicalisering. Waarom sommige Amsterdamse Moslims radicaal worden*. Amsterdam: Gemeente Amsterdam/IMES.

Toma, K. (2014). *Resilien-Tech. "Resilience-by-Design": Strategie für die technologischen Zukunftsthemen (Acatech Studie)*. Freiburg: Deutsche Akademie der Technikwissenschaften. Retrieved via http://www.bmbf.de/de/24434.php

Tugade, M. M., Fredrickson, B. L., & Barrett, L. F. (2004). "Psychological Resilience and Positive Emotional Granularity: Examining the Benefits of Positive Emotions on Coping and Health." *Journal of Personality*, 72.

van Eerten, J-J., Doosje, B., Konijn, E., de Graaf, B., & de Goede, M. (2017). *Developing a social media response to radicalization: The role of counter-narratives in prevention of radicalization and de-radicalization*. Amsterdam: University of Amsterdam, Department of Psychology.

Waller, M. A. (2001). Resilience in ecosystemic context: Evolution of the concept. *American Journal of Orthopsychiatry*, 71, 290–297.

Chapter 9

EXIT! The psychology of deradicalization and disengagement

Goals

- Examine the psychological processes of deradicalization and disengagement.
- Understand the role of trigger factors and resilience in deradicalization and disengagement.
- Outline the psychological processes that play a role in deradicalization and disengagement in the vulnerability phase, group phase, and action phase of our model of (de)radicalization.

Introduction

> If they want to make a difference in the world, they absolutely should not join the [extremist right-wing] movement. Do something different, but don't ask me what [...] That is something I have learned. You can find a subculture [in the extremist right-wing movement] full of aggression and problems and backstabbing. It is not worth the trouble. But where should you do it? That depends, I am still not a big fan of politics.
>
> Excerpt from an interview with a male Dutch former right-wing extremist
> (Feddes, Mann, & Doosje, 2013)

When asked what message he would send to young people who consider joining an extremist group to change society, this former right-wing extremist (who became a member of a right-wing extremist group when he was only 12) says it is of no use. Extremist groups, he says, are disorganized and rife with aggression and betrayal. After being a member of one of these groups for over 10 years, he became disappointed because another group member talked badly about him behind his back, which made him decide to leave the group when he was in his early 20s.

Can we say this person was deradicalized after this negative experience? How can we be sure? What events in a person's life lead to the decision to leave an extremist group? What, actually, do we mean by *deradicalization*? These are questions we address in this chapter. We first discuss the difference between two concepts that are at the core of this heated debate, disengagement and deradicalization. We then examine more closely which processes and trigger events can make a person decide to leave a group. We conclude with summarizing the most important psychological insights that are relevant to disengagement and deradicalization.

Disengagement versus deradicalization

When we talk about some individual being "deradicalized," we may have a clear idea about how this person *used to be* (as a radical) and *how he or she is now*. After being deradicalized, this person thinks, feels, and behaves very differently than before. However, just as someone is not radicalized in one instance – see also Chapter 4 – deradicalization is not a black-and-white, "either-or" phenomenon. Rather, it is a gradual process that usually starts with some event, idea, or insight (e.g., a *trigger*; see Chapter 7) and might result in a situation where the person is "back to normal" and part of the "mainstream" again. In between these extreme ends of the deradicalization spectrum, there are different stages to be discerned. For example, as the previous interview excerpt indicates, someone can no longer be part of a radical group (i.e., he or she is *disengaged* from the group) but still retain some radical ideas or identify to a certain extent with the group's ideology in a broader sense. Thus, this person cannot be considered (fully) deradicalized.

In our model presented at the start of this book (see Theoretical model on p. ix), we outlined both the process of radicalization and the process of deradicalization. The deradicalization process is indicated by the downward and horizontal arrows. Why the horizontal arrows in the three phases? This has to do with the distinction between *deradicalization* and *disengagement* (Schmid, 2013). *Disengagement* means that a person distances him- or herself from extremism in terms of their behavior. For example, the person leaves the radical group or stops being active in the group. *Deradicalization* goes a step further and implies that a person also denounces the values, attitudes, and views of the extremist group. Disengagement is largely about behavioral change that can be observed (i.e., a change in clothing, no longer interacting with extremist group members, no longer using threats or violence). Deradicalization is about behavioral change and, on top of that, about *cognition*: a change of a person's mind, which cannot be directly observed.

Taking the excerpt at the start of this chapter as an illustration, this person disengaged from the group, but it would go too far to conclude he (fully) deradicalized. This person left the extremist scene altogether to live a normal life without totally distancing himself from his personal ideology. Alternatively, a person who disengages from a particular extremist group may join another extremist group, thereby remaining "radical." In our model of radicalization, this is depicted by the horizontal arrows in the group phase and action phase.

Importantly, we do not consider a person in the vulnerability phase of our model of radicalization (see Chapter 4) radical. We therefore do not speak of *deradicalization* in regard to individuals in the vulnerability phase. The terms *deradicalization* and *disengagement* only refer to the group and action phase of the model. Intervention in the vulnerability phase is, therefore, actually referred to as *prevention* (see also Chapter 10, where we discuss how to deal best with radicalization).

This raises the question: To what extent do we want or expect individuals to change their ideological convictions when we talk about deradicalization? This question is actually the essence of a heated debate on what outcomes of counter-radicalization interventions ought to be. As discussed previously, it is important to note that a person may disengage from an extremist group while still maintaining extremist values, attitudes, and views. Indeed, research with former extremists suggests that disengagement without deradicalization is the rule rather than the exception (Horgan, 2008; Bjørgo, 2009). For example, based on interviews with former extremists, Horgan concludes (2008, p. 6):

> While almost all of the interviewees could be described as disengaged, not a single one of them could be said to be "deradicalized". In fact, even the process of disengagement was highly idiosyncratic for those interviewed. For some, leaving the movement was temporary, with members opting to come back to the movement at some later stage. Sometimes, this was to a different role, otherwise it was a return to the same role or function held before the initial departure.

This is also reflected in the statement at the start of this chapter of the former right-wing extremist we interviewed. He was strongly disappointed in the extremist group but still was not a big fan of other options (e.g., "politics") as the best way to counter perceived injustice. That disengagement does not necessarily imply a change in values, attitudes, and views is also illustrated in an interview with a former Moluccan-Dutch extremist in Box 9.1. In the next paragraphs, we describe in greater detail which events may cause an individual to disengage and/ or deradicalize and what psychological processes play a role.

Deradicalization step by step

While most psychological theoretical models deal with processes of radicalization, surprisingly little theoretical and empirical grounding exists for the psychological processes involved in deradicalization and disengagement (Mann, Nickolson, Feddes, Doosje, & Moghaddam, forthcoming). We argue that the same stages that we distinguished in our model of radicalization in Chapter 4 – in particular the group and action phase – can also be applied to deradicalization. This does not mean, however, that the causes of deradicalization – or their mirror images

Box 9.1 No regret

After World War II, the Netherlands was involved in a bloody struggle preceding the decolonization of Indonesia, which was under Dutch rule between 1816 and 1949. Moluccans, an ethnic group in Indonesia, fought on the Dutch side and were promised a free and independent Southern-Moluccan republic by the Dutch government. This promise was never fulfilled, however, causing anger among Moluccans who emigrated to the Netherlands after the decolonization of Indonesia. Prompted by this anger and frustration, Abé Sahetapy and six other Moluccans hijacked a train near Wijster, a little village in the East of the Netherlands, on December 2, 1975. The train operator and two passengers were killed in this action. After 12 days of negotiating, the hijackers surrendered. In an interview, the 57-year-old Abé, who at the time was 22 years old and was subsequently convicted for 14 years in prison for his participation in the action, describes the reasons for his involvement in the hijacking (Prillevitz, 2014). Abé describes how, before the hijacking, he found himself stuck between two cultures, the Dutch and Moluccan. He felt restless when he was an adolescent; one day he "kicked against one culture and the other day against the other." In terms of psychological needs (discussed in Chapter 5), he could perhaps best be described as having a need for a positive identity (his Moluccan identity being recognized) but also having a strong need for justice. "Our people were treated badly, and we did not accept that any longer." At the end of the interview, Abé is asked whether he regrets his deeds. He replies: "I do not regret the hijacking and still support it a hundred percent. The time I spent in prison was not a sacrifice for me. It was necessary, even though the hijacking did not result in anything concrete. Our actions did focus the attention on the Moluccan problem. Also, it resulted in more individual Moluccans to stand up for themselves after the 1970s. That is positive." He continues: "I still support [the cause], but now from a distance. I now would not hijack a train anymore because there is not a direct reason for it. At the time it was fitting though." We cannot say that Abé disengaged, as his terrorist group was neutralized. He did not purposefully leave the group. However, he still supports the cause and the use of violence at the time. As such, he is also not deradicalized.

– are always the same as those of radicalization. Sometimes, it does work that way. For example, increased trust in fellow group members will result in greater commitment to the group, but, as we will see later in this chapter, *reduced* trust in fellow group members can be a powerful reason for a person to leave the group. In contrast, feeling relatively deprived may play an important role in the decision to join an extremist group (i.e., Moghaddam, 2005), but reduced feelings of relative deprivation do not necessarily lead to the decision to leave an extremist group. In some respects, therefore, the process of deradicalization *mirrors* the process of radicalization, but that does not always have to be the case. A common thread that does run through both radicalization and deradicalization processes is that of the psychological needs described in Chapter 5. These needs, and the corresponding motivational imbalance, often precede the actual radicalization and often stay with the person during and after the process of disengagement and/or deradicalization.

In the discussion of deradicalization and disengagement, *resilience* plays a central role. As explained in Chapter 8 and depicted in our model at the start of the book (see p. ix), resilience can be viewed in two ways. First, individuals are more or less resilient against messages and ideologies from extremist groups. This applies particularly in the *vulnerability phase* and early on in the *group phase*. Second, once people have radicalized and are in the group or action phase, they may be more or less resilient *against messages from people outside of the terrorist group* to move away from the *action* and *group* phase. In this regard it is useful to make a distinction between "push" and "pull" forces when considering disengagement (Bjørgo, 2009, 2016). *Push factors* are negative events or situations in an extremist group that motivate an individual to leave the group. As we will see subsequently in the overview of trigger factors related to disengagement (Sections "Deradicalization and disengagement in the action phase" and "Deradicalization and disengagement in the group phase"), these push factors may be related to bad group functioning or misbehavior of individual members of the group. *Pull factors* are positive factors outside of the extremist group that motivate an individual to leave that group. Examples of these positive factors are the outlook of starting a family or career. In some cases, the criminal justice system may also provide positive pull factors, for example, by allowing former extremists to return to society and by offering amnesty and rehabilitation programs.

As we remarked earlier, psychological needs play a key role both in the radicalization and deradicalization processes. Propagandists and recruiters may purposefully aim at the needs of an individual to convince them of the extremist ideology and joining an extremist group. Once inside the group, exiting may be particularly difficult because of, for example, strong loyalty to group norms. Exiting may also be difficult because the group is fulfilling an individual's needs. For example, as reviewed in Chapters 5 and 6, the extremist group fulfils an important function in these phases, as it provides friendship, security, and social status (basic identity-related needs; Tajfel & Turner, 1979; Baumeister & Leary, 1995). Leaving the group, therefore, would mean *losing* group resources that meet these needs. In addition, the group can serve as a tool to counter perceived injustice (Van den Bos, 2018). Serving in the group can provide clear goals and give meaning to an individual's life, thereby meeting needs of significance (Kruglanski, Chen, Dechesne, Fishman, & Orehek, 2009). It can also meet a need for adventure and romanticism, which typify sensation seekers. Stepping out of the group, therefore, would imply a loss of significance. Alternatively, as the excerpt at the start of this chapter illustrated, if the group does not fulfill the needs of an individual anymore, this may result in disillusionment and motivate a person to disengage from the group. Clearly, the earlier-mentioned push and pull factors are strongly related to the psychological needs of a person.

One of the main goals of interventions aimed at supporting people to disengage from extremist groups is, therefore, to help people who want to leave an extremist group to find alternative ways to fulfill their basic needs (see also Chapter 10 for a more detailed discussion). This is illustrated by the following excerpt of a former right-wing extremist we interviewed (Feddes et al., 2013, p. 64):

> I think that each person has a unique need. Sometimes work could do the trick. Or a house, getting to know other people, start a social life outside the group. [...] You have to get to know them really well. [...] Some really believe strongly [in the group ideology]. I think you need a person they can trust, a person from the outside.

EXIT programs such as that initiated by Tore Bjørgo in Norway that can now be found in different countries, including Germany, Denmark, and the Netherlands, aim at supporting individuals' disengagement from extremist groups by helping them find new housing or a (new) job or enroll in education (Bjørgo & Carlsson, 2005; see Figure 9.1).

So why do individuals disengage or deradicalize in the action and group phase? And why do individuals become less sensitive to radicalization? In the next three sections, we discuss the psychological processes involved in each phase, starting with the action phase. As we will see, trigger factors, defined in Chapter 7 as observable events outside an individual which can lead to further (de)radicalization, often play an important role.

Figure 9.1 The logo from EXIT Deutschland, an organization that focuses on helping individuals leaving extremist groups. (From https://www.exit-deutschland.de.)

Deradicalization and disengagement in the action phase

Why do individuals abstain from taking (violent) action? In the action phase of radicalization, intervention from outside the radical group is most difficult because groups are close-knit and group members are usually strongly determined in their goals. It is at this stage that extremists have received training, have been inspired by others (copy-cat behavior), or act on "calls for attacks" by group leaders (Feddes, Nickolson, & Doosje, 2015b). They are, therefore, motivated and willing to carry out terrorist attacks. What may change these people's minds?

First, an ideology can help individuals to perceive violence as the only means to reach important group goals (see also Chapter 6). In the action phase, people usually see no alternative options anymore. A *change in this perceived necessity of acting and/or the offer of alternatives for violence* may therefore be effective in changing this perception. For example, by engaging terrorist groups in political negotiations, the violent goals of the group may be "neutralized" and the felt necessity of action may be lowered (Moghaddam, 2009).

Second, an *experience with violence* may also be a trigger factor making an individual disengage from a group. For example, Demant, Slootman, Buijs, and Tillie (2008) describe how some members of a squatter group disengaged after the more extreme members of the group had decided to start using violence against the police.

Third, *confrontations with authorities* can also motivate a person in the action phase to disengage from a radical group. For instance, Slootman, Tillie, Majdy, and Buijs (2009) describe that one of the young Salafi Jihadi men they interviewed mentioned that he distanced himself from the group because "he did not want anything to do with the AIVD [Dutch Intelligence Service]" (p. 20). Governmental security measures may, therefore, act as a trigger factor leading to disengagement. The perception that authorities are capable and effective in countering extremist acts can increase stress in members of extremist groups who feel themselves targeted. A continuous surveillance of police and security services can wear out individuals and feed the motivation to lead a "normal life." In regard to counter-radicalization interventions, then, it is important to be ready at that moment to offer support needed for the individual to leave the group. In an interview we conducted with a former right-wing extremist in 2013, this person explained that when he was arrested, he felt totally isolated: "In that prison cell I started to think about wat I was doing. I realised I was really on the way down. For me that was the moment to step out of the scene." The availability of EXIT options, as discussed earlier, may provide the last "pull" out of the extremist scene.

Fourth, *disappointment in the group* is a strong trigger for an individual to disengage from the group in this phase. The social support of fellow groupmates may serve as a catalyst for people to carry out the task at hand and also help to create a *diffusion of responsibility* for the violence used. Disillusionment in the group not being able to "put their money where their mouth is" and provide the support needed or carry out the attack may result in a reduced trust in group members and the group as a whole, which may eventually lead to disengagement (Bjørgo, 2009).

In sum, in the action phase, disengagement can come about through a change in perceived necessity of violence (through political negotiations), own direct experiences with violence that result in a re-evaluation of the necessity of violence, confrontations with authorities, and a disappointment in the group or its members.

Deradicalization and disengagement in the group phase

The group phase is particularly notable for the development of strong attitudes and individuals becoming increasingly attached to the terrorist group. The basis for categorization of the in-group against the out-group ("us versus them thinking") and the perceived moral superiority of the in-group are established in this phase (see Chapter 4). Attitudes supporting the ideology of the group are strengthened through group processes such as *group think* and *polarization*, as discussed in Chapter 6. In this phase, strong social norms are introduced that prevent individuals from leaving the group. Also, "bridge burning," or the breaking of bonds with people (family, friends) outside of the extremist group are trigger factors that often take place in this phase (see Chapter 4 and Chapter 7).

In the group phase, similar processes as described in the action phase can play a role in the decision for a person to disengage. An individual may start to doubt his or her identification with a group as a consequence of violence, intervention of authorities, or misbehavior of fellow group members that results in increased doubt about the functioning and efficacy of the group. For example, one former right-wing extremist we interviewed mentioned the following (Feddes et al., 2013, p. 57):

> So much rivalry and frustration exist between [different right-wing extremist groups], that is also the main reason why [extreme right] never became big in the Netherlands. Combat 18 could not get along with Blood & Honour. And Blood & Honour couldn't get along with the nationalists. There was no cooperation.

The perceived inefficacy of the group was for this person an important reason for leaving the group. Just as in the action phase, misbehavior of group members is also often mentioned as playing a role (Feddes et al., 2013, p. 57):

> It was terribly amateuristic, so many screw-ups. There were so many morons within the scene, who pulled everything apart. You could reason with one person, but if he had been drinking that same person was terrible. And that is how it went in many groups; they all had one idiot who screwed up.

In addition to these factors, positive contact with out-group members may be powerful in setting in motion a deradicalization process in the group phase.

Sieckelinck and colleagues give the example of a right-wing extremist whose brother had a girlfriend with a migrant background (Sieckelinck, Sikkens, Van San, Kotnis, & De Winter, 2019). The positive interactions with this girl changed his view of "the enemy." Also, Altier, Thoroughgood, and Horgan (2014) describe that positive experiences with individuals outside of the extremist group with moderate views may make a person question his or her involvement in the group. A change of norms in the group, introduced by alternative views or less extreme group members, can play an important role in this respect.

Sometimes *specific individuals (former friends, family, colleagues) outside the group* may help in the decision to leave an extremist group. As the following former right-wing extremist put it in an interview (Feddes et al., 2013, p. 58):

> I had a very good friend. We had lost touch but eventually we got into contact again. It was my old neighbour and he had been my best friend, kind of a brother to me. That contact became stronger again. So, besides my group of friends [who were all in the right-wing extremist movement] I had this friend whom I could trust, he was an anchor for me. [When I quit the group] at least he was there. Social isolation is a big problem. Everything, your whole social life is about the friends you have in the [right-wing extremist] group. It does not matter if it is a movement, or ideology, it is all about that group.

Leaving an extremist group can result in a complete loss of social life. Having friends outside of the group whom one can trust may, therefore, be an important "catalyst" in the process of leaving the group.

Other factors that play a role are related to an increased motivation for a "normal" life. A *marriage* can induce a person to disengage from an extremist group. For some individuals, the thought of having to leave their family behind to join the Jihad was decisive in not radicalizing further (Altier et al., 2014). For example, Sterkenburg (2014) describes the case of Victor D., who had plans to join the Jihad and did not want to marry for this reason. *Becoming a parent* can also be a turning point, as such an event can give new meaning to a person's life, and the anticipation of losing a connection with the child can make an individual move away from extremism (Sieckelinck & De Winter, 2015). Indeed, studies on crime show that marriage and becoming a parent are often turning points in a criminal career (Zoutewelle-Terovan, Van der Geest, Liefbroer, & Bijleveld, 2014) and result in decreased involvement in youth gangs (Tripp, 2007).

In sum, in the group phase, disengagement can come about through similar factors as in the action phase (change in perceived necessity of violence, direct experiences with violence, confrontations with authorities, disappointment in the group or its members). In addition, positive contact with out-group members, an important individual outside of the group who convinces a person to change direction, and changes in the personal life (marriage, becoming a parent) are important factors.

Preventing radicalization in the vulnerability phase

In this stage, we find individuals who are exploring opportunities to counter perceived injustice and who become increasingly frustrated by the limited avenues of doing so. Important psychological mechanisms that play a role here are feelings of *relative deprivation* and *extreme negative emotions* (shame, hate, humiliation), which may be caused by events in the direct environment and worldwide (i.e., the wars in the Middle East; see Kruglanski & Fishman, 2009), and *identity-related issues* such as a perceived lack of significance or a goal in life, not knowing where to belong, feeling in between two cultures, or experiencing a threat to the in-group.

Countering perceptions of injustice may be effective in reducing vulnerability for radicalization. Importantly, research on crime has convincingly shown that *being employed* or having an *education* can be strong protective factors against delinquent behavior (Van der Geest, Bijleveld, & Blokland, 2011; Blomberg, Bales, & Piquero, 2012). Helping individuals get a job or education may be, therefore, a powerful measure in reducing vulnerability for radicalization.

An increase in *self-esteem* (having a positive self-view) and *self-efficacy* (in this case referring to being able to finish an education, find a job, or have perspective in life) may help to prevent radicalization (Feddes, Mann, & Doosje, 2015a).

Increasing *knowledge*, *empathy*, and *perspective taking* are also effective in creating more moderate and nuanced views toward authorities, institutions, and out-groups. In doing so, vulnerability for radicalization can be reduced. An increase in knowledge about democracy, for example, has been found to be associated with more positive attitudes toward democracy in adolescents and young adults (Feddes, Huijzer, Van Ooijen, & Doosje, 2019).

Just as in the group phase, intergroup contact is another important avenue for reducing the likelihood an individual will radicalize. More than half a century of research on the intergroup contact hypothesis has shown that *contact with out-group members* can result in more positive attitudes toward out-groups through increased knowledge, empathy, and perspective taking (Allport, 1954; Pettigrew, 1998; Pettigrew & Tropp, 2006). It is not even necessary to have direct contact; knowing that other in-group members have positive contact experiences with out-group members, also called *extended contact*, can already result in more positive intergroup attitudes (Wright, Aron, McLaughlin-Volpe, & Ropp, 1997). This has been shown, for example, in the context of religious tension in Northern Ireland, where both direct and extended contact reduced negative feelings between Catholic republicans and Protestant loyalists and increased trust in out-group members (Paolini, Hewstone, Cairns, & Voci, 2004; Tam, Hewstone, Kenworthy, & Cairns, 2009). While in the group phase, individuals may be more resilient against these "contact effects," in the vulnerability phase, these may be particularly effective.

In sum, in the vulnerability phase, in particular, factors at the individual (micro) level play a role. Increasing self-esteem, reducing feelings of injustice (i.e., through education, a job, having a positive outlook on life), creating empathy and perspective taking, education in the political system, and learning how to deal with negative emotions and insecurities related to identity are important in preventing radicalization.

Summary

In this chapter, we explained the concept of deradicalization and how this differs from disengagement. Most people who are in the process of deradicalization actually do not fully deradicalize, but they merely disengage from the radical group and cease to use violence or perform other actions in the name of the group. Thus, their behavior changes, but they may still endorse (some part of) the group ideology. In our model of radicalization presented at the start of this book, this is depicted by the horizontal arrows in the group and action phase (see Theoretical model on p. ix).

We outlined some of the specific processes that play a role in deradicalization and disengagement in the action phase and the group phase and the processes that can prevent radicalization in the vulnerability phase. In the action and group phases, trigger factors such as the misbehavior of group members, misfunctioning of the group, positive contact with out-group members, or a change in perceived necessity of using violence may counter processes of radicalization and result in disengagement and, possibly, deradicalization. In the vulnerability phase, factors that play an important role in preventing radicalization are mainly situated at an individual level (i.e., creating self-esteem, providing a positive outlook on life, learning to deal well with negative emotions and insecurities related to identity), but also education (i.e., learning about the democratic system) and intergroup contact are deemed particularly effective in this phase.

The research on processes of deradicalization and disengagement is still in its infancy compared to research and theorizing on radicalization. It is, however, important to realize that the process of deradicalization is not necessarily the opposite of the process of radicalization. In each phase, specific psychological processes play a role in changing people's minds away from violent ideologies and prevent them from joining a radical group or lead them to leave extremism behind.

Recommended reading

Schmid, A. P. (2013). Radicalisation, de-radicalisation, counter-radicalisation: A conceptual discussion and literature review. *ICCT Research Paper*, March 2013, available at: http://www.icct.nl.

In this paper, Alex Schmid provides a critical review of theoretical concepts related to radicalization, deradicalization, and disengagement, and reviews relevant literature.

References

Allport, G. W. (1954). *The nature of prejudice*. Cambridge, MA: Addison-Wesley.

Altier, M. B., Thoroughgood, C. N., & Horgan, J. G. (2014). Turning away from terrorism: Lessons from psychology, sociology, and criminology. *Journal of Peace Research*, 51(5), 647–661.

Baumeister, R. F., & Leary, M. R. (1995). The need to belong: desire for interpersonal attachments as a fundamental human motivation. *Psychological Bulletin*, 117, 497–529.

Bjørgo, T. (2009). Processes of disengagement from violent groups of the extreme right. In: T. Bjørgo, & J. Horgan (Eds.), *Leaving terrorism behind: Individual and collective disengagement*. Abingdon: Routledge.

Bjørgo, T. (2016). Counter-terrorism as crime prevention: a holistic approach. *Behavioral Sciences of Terrorism and Political Aggression*, 8(1), 25–44.

Bjørgo, T., & Carlsson, Y. (2005). *Early intervention with violent and racist youth groups*. Oslo: Norwegian Institute of International Affairs.

Blomberg, T. G., Bales, W. D., & Piquero, A. R. (2012). Is educational achievement a turning point for incarcerated delinquents across race and sex? *Journal of Youth and Adolescence*, 41, 202–216.

Demant, F., Slootman, M., Buijs, F., & Tillie, J. (2008). *Teruggang en uittreding. Processen van de-radicalisering ontleed [Disengagement. Processes of de-radicalization explained]*. Amsterdam: IMES.

Feddes, A. R., Mann, L., & Doosje, B. (2013). *Empirical study as part of a scientific approach to finding indicators of and responses to radicalization (SAFIRE)*. Report presented to the European Commission.

Feddes, A. R., Mann, L., & Doosje, B. (2015a). Increasing self-esteem and empathy to prevent violent radicalization: a longitudinal quantitative evaluation of a resilience training focused on adolescents with a dual identity. *Journal of Applied Social Psychology*, 45(7), 400–411.

Feddes, A. R., Nickolson, L., & Doosje, B. (2015b). *Triggerfactoren in het radicaliseringsproces [Trigger factors in the radicalization process]*. The Hague/Amsterdam: Expertise-unit Sociale Stabiliteit/University of Amsterdam.

Feddes, A. R., Huijzer, A., Van Ooijen, I., & Doosje, B. (2019). Fortress of democracy: engaging youngsters in democracy results in more support for the political system. *Peace and Conflict: Journal of Peace Psychology*, 25, 158–164.

Horgan, J. (2008). De-radicalization or disengagement? A process in need of clarity and a counterterrorism initiative in need of evaluation. *Perspectives on Terrorism*, 2(4), 3–8.

Kruglanski, A. W., & Fishman, S. (2009). Psychological factors in terrorism and counterterrorism: individual, group, and organizational levels of analysis. *Social Issues and Policy Review*, 3, 1–44.

Kruglanski, A. W., Chen, X., Dechesne, M., Fishman, S., & Orehek, E. (2009). Fully committed: suicide bombers' motivation and the quest for personal significance. *Political Psychology*, 30(3), 331–357.

Mann, L., Nickolson, L., Feddes, A. R., Doosje, B., & Moghaddam, F. M. (forthcoming). Exploring the Viability of Phase-Based Models to (De)Radicalization. In: S. Lid, & S. Hansen (Eds.), *Routledge handbook on de-radicalization*.

Moghaddam, F. M. (2005). The staircase to terrorism: A psychological exploration. *American Psychologist*, 60(2), 161–169.

Moghaddam, F. M. (2009). De-radicalization and the Staircase from Terrorism. In: D. Canter (Ed.), *The faces of terrorism: multidisciplinary perspectives* (pp. 277–292). John Wiley & Sons Ltd.

Paolini, S., Hewstone, M., Cairns, E., & Voci, A. (2004). Effects of direct and indirect cross-group friendships on judgments of Catholics and Protestants in Northern Ireland: The mediating role of an anxiety-reduction mechanism. *Personality and Social Psychology Bulletin*, 30, 770–786.

Pettigrew, T. F. (1998). Intergroup contact theory. *Annual Review of Psychology*, 49, 65–85.

Pettigrew, T. F., & Tropp, L. R. (2006). A meta-analytic test of intergroup contact theory. *Journal of Personality and Social Psychology*, 90, 751–783.

Prillevitz, P. (2014). Interview ex-treinkaper Sahetapy [Interview ex-hijacker Sahetapy]. *Historien*, October 16, 2014. Obtained from: http://www.historien.nl.

Schmid, A. P. (2013). Radicalisation, de-radicalisation, counter-radicalisation: a conceptual discussion and literature review. *ICCT Research Paper*, March 2013, available at: http://www.icct.nl.

Sieckelinck, S., & De Winter, M. (2015). *Formers & families: Transitional journeys in and out of extremism in the UK, Denmark and The Netherlands*. The Hague: NCTV.

Sieckelinck, S., Sikkens, E., Van San, M., Kotnis, S. & De Winter, M. (2019). Transitional journeys into and out of extremism. A biographical approach. *Studies in Conflict and Terrorism*, 42, 662–682.

Slootman, M., Tillie, J., Majdy, A., & Buijs, F. (2009). *Salafi-jihadi's in Amsterdam [Salafi-Jihadis in Amsterdam]. FORUM: Reeks Religie en Samenleving*. Amsterdam: Uitgeverij Aksant.

Sterkenburg, N. (2014). *Hoe een postbode strijder in Syrië werd [How a postman became warrior in Syria]*. Elsevier.

Tam, T., Hewstone, M., Kenworthy, J., & Cairns, E. (2009). Intergroup trust in Northern Ireland. *Personality and Social Psychology Bulletin*, 35(1), 45–59.

Tajfel, H., & Turner, J. C. (1979). An integrative theory of intergroup conflict. In: W. G. Austin, & S. Worchel (Eds.), *The social psychology of intergroup relations* (pp. 33–47). Monterey, CA: Brooks/Cole.

Tripp, B. G. (2007). Fatherhood and crime: examining life course transitions among men in Harlem. *Doctoral dissertation*, University of Florida.

Van den Bos, K. (2018). *Why people radicalize: How unfairness judgements are used to fuel radical beliefs, extremist behaviors, and terrorism*. Oxford University Press.

Van der Geest, V. R., Bijleveld, C. C., & Blokland, A. J. (2011). The effects of employment on longitudinal trajectories of offending: a follow-up of high-risk youth from 18 to 32 years of age. *Criminology*, 49, 1195–234.

Wright, S. C., Aron, A., McLaughlin-Volpe, T., & Ropp, S. A. (1997). The extended contact effect: Knowledge of cross-group friendships and prejudice. *Journal of Personality and Social Psychology*, 73(1), 73.

Zoutewelle-Terovan, M., Van der Geest, V., Liefbroer, A., & Bijleveld, C. (2014). Criminality and family formation: effects of marriage and parenthood on criminal behavior for men and women. *Crime & Delinquency*, 60, 1209–1234.

Chapter 10

Eight lessons for dealing with radicalization

Introduction

The previous chapters have shown how to think and talk about radicalization as a psychological process but did not explicitly answer the question of what to do about it. At the same time, the analysis of a problem – to the extent that we can call radicalization a problem – is absolutely essential as a starting point for thinking about solutions. It not only enables us to better detect radicalization but also helps us to counter it by pointing to various factors and phases in this process and steers us away from futile or even counterproductive measures we might be inclined to take.

In this chapter, we spell out eight important lessons (see Box 10.1) that can be drawn from our model of radicalization as presented at the start of this book (see p. ix). To make these lessons as concrete as possible, the specific psychological perspective of this book is complemented by insights from other scientific disciplines (such as political and pedagogical sciences), as well as experiences from local practices. To be sure, these lessons do not amount to clear-cut solutions. If there is one thing that can be learned from this book, it is that such solutions do not exist (see Lesson 1). But the eight lessons will help professionals that are regularly

---

Box 10.1   Eight lessons for dealing with radicalization

1. Realize that radicalization is complex but not exotic
2. Know your problems and dilemmas
3. Get out, connect, and (net)work together
4. Make a thorough analysis of the risks of radicalization
5. Keep your eye on the needs
6. Resilience, resilience, resilience
7. Have a compelling story – but know when to tell it
8. Keep doing your job, and do it well

confronted with radicalization – such as civil servants, care workers, and police officers – to navigate this issue in an informed and effective way.

Lesson 1: Realize that radicalization is complex but not exotic

When viewed as a whole, the bigger picture that emerges from the chapters of this book is that of radicalization as a complex phenomenon. A multitude of (trigger) events, processes, and circumstances have to come together in a very specific way to end up with the "cocktail" of radicalization. This means that one should be wary of simple explanations that point to a single cause, such as economic hardship, feelings of injustice, a longing for thrills, or even a radical doctrine itself (see Box 10.2). Likewise, models that envision radicalization as a very linear and deterministic process should be viewed with suspicion, as individuals can go back and forth between different degrees of radicalization and often do not even reach the fatal action stage. In sum, there is no "radical-whisperer" that somehow possesses intimate knowledge of the one thing that truly moves the radicalizing individual. Similarly, we cannot draw up Wild Wild West wanted posters with a fixed set of characteristics that would help us to apprehend "the radical." Unfortunately for those working at the frontlines of radicalization, there is no miracle cure to be found.

But there is also no need for despair. The emerging picture of radicalization shows us that this process is made up of factors that are very recognizable for local practitioners. They regularly encounter phenomena such as job dismissals, encounters with discrimination, and domestic violence. They already have experience with heated discussions about religion and politics in the classroom or the community center and might have already seen how people – especially younger people – are capable of holding extreme views and undertaking radical action when pressured by peers. Most importantly, they know that what drives all of us are basic human needs for belonging, justice, significance, and sensation. It is all a matter of recognizing when these needs push someone off the rails and knowing what to do to get them back on track.

Box 10.2   Recognizing complexity in national policy

As a government, it is important not only to acknowledge radicalization's complexity but also to act accordingly. As a study shows, countries like the United Kingdom, Denmark, and the Netherlands frequently pay lip service to the complexity of the radicalization process: they say that radicalization consists of many different factors, but in practice often choose a few of them to focus on in their preventative measures against radicalization – without justification of this choice (Hardy, 2018).

Lesson 2: Know your problem and dilemmas

When we say that a radical person is derailed or deranged, we are making a normative statement. This forces us to answer the question of precisely which "rails" we are talking about. What is problematic about radicalization? Couldn't it actually be something positive? Weren't Martin Luther King and Mandela also considered radicals? As we have emphasized in Chapter 1, radicalization is often a very subjective and value-loaded term, where it depends on the point of reference whether a specific form of radicalization is denounced as problematic. We are, therefore, faced with a challenge, as thinking about solutions is only possible if we know exactly what the problem is. Arguably, the objective psychological perspective employed in this book does not help us much further in answering this question.

This does not mean that all is relative, however, and that we are stuck in a Babylonian confusion of tongues. In fact, common grounds already exist and just need some work to be articulated and specified. For many governments, for example, the obvious point of reference is that of liberal democracy: a political system that enables groups with different ways of life to settle their differences in a fair and peaceful way. From this perspective, ideals and actions that demonstrably lead or amount to violence are (obviously) problematic. But even if there is no direct link with violence, radical groups could be argued to be problematic from a democratic perspective if they erode or undermine democratic values or the democratic process. For example, they might silence or intimidate others in their community or neighborhood, stir up hatred, or actively reject the democratic system (and stimulate others to do the same). As these actions differ in the severity of their impact – not all are equally problematic or urgent – they might also demand more or less severe countermeasures. Youth workers and teachers are, in a sense, also bound by this liberal democratic frame of reference, but they also have their own pedagogical perspective. From such a perspective, radical thoughts and behavior can be problematic if they threaten a healthy social or emotional development or jeopardize the pedagogical or educational relationship with upbringers or educators (Sieckelinck, Sikkens, Van San, Kotnis, & De Winter, 2019).

While these perspectives are helpful and practical, they also present us with unavoidable dilemmas. Radical thoughts and ideals might be problematic from a democratic or pedagogical perspective, but they also – potentially, at least – form an indispensable part of stable democracies and a healthy social and emotional development. Democracies are designed to allow for a wide range of worldviews, even radical ones. And the adoption of extreme ideals is part and parcel of many an adolescence – it is often what allows individuals to grow and ultimately become more stable and "mature." Determining whether and to which degree radical thoughts and behavior are problematic and should be countered therefore means that one must constantly balance these conflicting considerations.

Lesson 3: Get out, connect, and (net)work together

The realization that radicalization is a complex and multifaceted problem goes hand in hand with the realization that, as a local practitioner, you only hold one piece of the puzzle. Radicalization cannot be prevented solely by teachers, youth workers or police officers, and parents, or preachers. It demands a joint effort, and this can only come about if all the relevant parties get out and connect.

A common thread through this book has been that radicalization is best conceived of in terms of intergroup relations and closely connected to broader social tensions. This means that, when looking for societal partners as a governmental organization or a professional, it is important to cast the net as widely as possible. One should not only approach the community where radicalization seems most urgent, as one type of radicalism could easily provoke or "trigger" another – think of the rise of right-wing radicalism as a response to Islamic radicalism, and vice versa. Furthermore, a focus on "usual suspects" should be avoided; an exclusive focus on (potentially) radical groups or radical individuals overlooks the fact that more "moderate" groups and individuals can just as easily become affected by resulting social tensions and could also play an important role in mitigating them.

"Go out and connect" might seem obvious or superfluous, but it is often harder than one might expect. Based also on the findings in this book (see Chapters 5 and 8, for example), one can expect strong emotions – or even seemingly impenetrable inverted shields of resilience – when addressing radical views or related social tensions. In less extreme cases, a certain level of distrust of government officials or other professionals might exist, or the persons or organizations in question might just have a very different analysis of what the "problem" of radicalization is. This is all the more urgent when considering that mutual trust and a shared vision and purpose are essential for an effective collaboration. When forging a partnership, then, one of the first things to do is have an open and honest talk about each other's goals and idea(l)s and the role each partner would play. For governments, this also means dealing with fundamental dilemmas (see Box 10.3).

There are many reasons partnerships come into being; many ways in which networks of institutions, organizations, and individuals could address the issue of radicalization. It could be to present a united front against certain radical or extremist ideas, to build bridges between different groups, to build trust and to legitimize government policy, but also to gather information and intelligence or to intervene in specific radicalization processes (Stephens & Sieckelinck, 2019). Each of these purposes may very well call for different types of expertise that are needed and different kinds of actors (i.e., first-line workers, police, policy makers, etc.) that need to be involved. In each case, building such networks is absolutely necessary for any attempt of countering radicalization to be effective (see also Eijkman & Roodnat, 2017) – which will become clearer in the following lessons.

Box 10.3   Dilemmas in engaging with local communities

The study "Engaging with Violent Islamic Extremism" by Bovenkerk and Vermeulen (2012) analyzes local anti-radicalization policies in the Western European cities of London, Paris, Amsterdam, Berlin, and Antwerp. It roughly distinguishes three dilemmas these cities have had to grapple with in their engagement with local Islamic communities. First, there is the dilemma of defining who the enemy is, which is strongly related to the dilemma discussed in Lesson 1 in this chapter. If it chooses to work with (non-violent) radical, fundamentalist, or orthodox organizations, the government may undermine their own liberal-democratic values, but excluding these organizations might make its anti-radicalization policies distinctly less effective. A second dilemma has to do with representation: when authorities want to engage with the Islamic population through certain organizations, they want these organizations to represent the community. At the same time, they know that these communities are not coherent and can never be represented fully. By selecting some organizations and not others, they can even alter the power relations within the community, which might be the last thing the government wants. The third and final dilemma concerns the government's modus operandi: if the government chooses to publicly engage with radical organizations – for instance, through debates – it may be able to better contrast its own message against that of the radical organization and perhaps convince moderate citizens not to join that group. At the same time, by engaging with them, it also provides a platform for radical organizations to broadcast their message, which might undermine the government's views and policies.

Lesson 4: Make a thorough analysis of the risks of radicalization

Before taking any measures to counter or prevent radicalization, it is wise to analyze what the risks of radicalization are. And just as Chapter 3 showed how a combination of different methods is most effective when studying radicalization, different sources and types of knowledge are also needed when taking stock of the risks of radicalization in a specific context – whether it is on an individual level or a more aggregate level such as a neighborhood or a city. The type of information that is needed also depends on which phase of radicalization we are talking about: the vulnerability phase, the group phase, or the action phase.

To estimate whether people could be at risk of becoming vulnerable to radical groups and ideologies, one could first look at structural conditions and general characteristics that might, as mentioned in Chapter 4, provide the "background music" to radicalization: socioeconomic status, gender, education, and so forth. Such information is relatively easily to find, whether it is on an individual level or neighborhood level. At the same time, the relation between such factors and radicalization is rather weak, as was also explained in Chapter 5. We would, therefore, do better to complement this information by considering certain trigger factors that can be associated with vulnerability to radicalization. Chapter 7 showed how such triggers are often events like domestic conflicts, encounters with discrimination, the death of a loved one, run-ins with the authorities, and being dismissed from work or school. Information about the occurrence of such events on a neighborhood or municipality level may be available in police files, unemployment numbers, or reports on local discrimination. Youth workers, teachers, and other professionals might be aware of such events in individual cases – especially if they are in touch and exchange knowledge with each other.

The risks of people entering the group phase of radicalization are harder to estimate. Since joining a radical group, meeting a radical person, and burning bridges are important triggers here, one would need to know, for example, whether there are radical persons present in the neighborhood and whether there are nearby radical groups that increasingly isolate themselves from society. Or, even more complicated, one would need to know what kind of websites, online fora, or app groups are visited by the individual(s) in question. Such information can only be gathered through networks that are sufficiently rooted in society. This leaves aside, of course, techniques and methods used by police and intelligence agencies. These can be used for analyzing the group phase but are perhaps most relevant in the action stage. In this final phase, detailed and privileged data from police and intelligence sources may reveal how radicalized individuals become more intent on using violence, gain the capability to do so (through training, for example), and plan their attack (Gill, Corner, McKee, Hitchen, & Betley, 2019).

It is important to note that making risk assessments is very challenging (see Box 10.4) and can also create new risks. As became clear in Chapter 4 about phase models, radicalizing individuals do not all necessarily end up in the final action phase. Their trajectory can be very ad hoc, take a long time, and be dynamic – meaning that they could just as well desist or deradicalize instead of radicalizing further. Assessing individuals based on the risks they pose may lead to a very distorted image as to what the urgency of the threat is and may very well lead to individuals being targeted who were not going to pose any threat but do end up radicalizing further because of premature actions on the side of government or police.

Lesson 5: Keep your eye on the needs

One of the most central points of this book is that, in the end, radicalization is driven by an imbalance of needs, where one need is so strong that it is conducive to radical (or other destructive) behavior. This insatiable need could be more or

Box 10.4 The method – and challenges – of risk assessment methods

It is one thing for a local government to estimate whether a certain area could be fertile ground for radicalization, gathering statistical and (other) relatively accessible information about topics such as discrimination, criminality, domestic violence, general wellbeing, and perceived tensions. It is a whole different thing to assess whether a specific individual is a concrete risk or threat to others. There are models to assess such risks when it comes to issues such as work-related violence, sexual violence, and fire setting, but understanding and managing the risks of violence by radicalized individuals is especially complex (Logan & Lloyd, 2018). First, there are many different types of harmful outcomes to be considered – not only executing violence but also supporting it, for example. Second, the process of radicalization is complex and the empirical scientific work relatively scarce, which means that there is simply not enough evidence to tie certain factors to a specific degree (or type) or risk. And third, the context in which the assessment takes place is very complex (Sarma, 2017). Not only the societal context, where social, political, economic, religious, cultural, and historical factors interact, but also the professional context, where there are many different agencies that have access to different sources that are relevant to risk assessment and that each have their own ways of working and looking at the world. Moreover, the process takes place in real time, often based on a narrow selection of information, from sources that may not be credible (Logan & Lloyd, 2018).

The implication of the previous is that, first, a high level of multidisciplinary and multi-agency cooperation is required. Second, the assessment of extremist violence has to be discretional, which means that there cannot be any direct line between the gathered data and the judgment. The risk cannot be "calculated" by interpreting "complete" data through fixed and explicit rules, yielding unquestionable results. At the most, practitioners can apply general guidelines to incomplete and flawed evidence, which means that they have to use their judgment and discretion to produce a credible assessment (Logan & Lloyd, 2018). At the moment, there are four tools that can help them make such an assessment: the VERA-2R, the ERG-22+, the Multi-Level Guidelines, and the Terrorist Radicalisation Assessment Protocol-18 (TRAP-18), which are publicly available. But much hinges on the persons that are involved, then, and the degree to which they are sufficiently capable and knowledgeable. In fact, for a more thorough and reliable assessment, it is important that these practitioners be specially trained for this purpose (Eijkman & Roodnat, 2017; Geurts et al., 2017).

less innate, or it could be caused by a specific trigger event in one's personal life. In each case, it plays a role throughout the whole process of radicalization and deradicalization, so it is important to keep one's eye on these needs at all times.

There are different ways to deal with these needs. Addressing the motivational imbalance through psychological or psychiatric help seems like an obvious route, especially when the situation is urgent. One could also accept that a certain imbalance will always be there and find different ways of satisfying the need in question. For justice seekers in the vulnerability phase, for example, this could mean providing them with alternative ways of venting their feelings of injustice, through debates at school or in the neighborhood, or translating these feelings into constructive action through political parties or movements. Thrill seekers could be offered opportunities to practice extreme sports, and civil society organizations, sports clubs, or community centers could be a safe harbor for identity seekers looking for somewhere to belong. Support to deal with these strong needs could also be given by role models or mentors, which is a frequently used method in radicalization programs as well as other preventative policies in the social domain (see Box 10.5).

Finally, as we have seen in Chapter 9, the absence of the satisfaction of needs is an important reason for leaving a radical group. Radical individuals often become disillusioned when their group does not live up to their expectations and does not provide what they were looking for. Justice seekers may discover that most of the members of their right-wing group are more interested in enjoying themselves than in political action or discern an unpalatable hypocrisy in their leaders. Identity-seekers can become increasingly disappointed in the quality of social relations within the group, significance seekers might find the group's ideology unbearably superficial, and thrill seekers may just find the life in their radical milieu plain

Box 10.5   Steering clear from radicalization: Mentors as guides

Mentors play an important role in the process of deradicalization. As Garfinkel states, "change often hinges on a relationship with a mentor or friend who supports and affirms peaceful behavior" (Garfinkel, 2007; see also Altier et al., 2014). Moreover, mentors can prove to be crucial in steering vulnerable individuals clear from radical ideologies and toward other ways of satisfying their needs. They can stimulate connection with diverse peers to provide a sense of belonging and identity, they can question or redirect feelings of injustice, and they can boost confidence that may lead to an occupation (employment, education) that gives the individual a feeling of significance (DuBois & Alem, 2017). They can thereby also contribute to the individual's resilience (see Lesson 6).

boring. It is this disillusionment that can be seized as an opportunity to direct radical individuals away from their group or even stimulated; one could discredit the leader by questioning their ideological commitment, drive a wedge between different members of a radical group, provide alternative sources of significance, or (re)connect the radical individuals with their families or other places they may belong. Given the fact that intervening in the later group and action phases is especially hard – see Chapter 9 and Lesson 7 – it is even more important to be there and address these needs when the persons in question show doubts or lean toward leaving the group.

Lesson 6: Resilience, resilience, resilience

Simply put, the reason people do not radicalize despite the attractiveness of radical groups and ideologies is because they are resilient. It is therefore not surprising that resilience occupies a central place in many programs that focus on preventing radicalization and extremism. It is a notion that allows for a positive and constructive approach to this urgent issue and is familiar to professionals that work on similar or related social issues like the prevention of addiction and crime. At the same time, as we have seen in Chapter 8, it is a concept that is notoriously difficult to define. In Chapter 9, we therefore proposed a concept of resilience against radicalization that is both compatible with existing knowledge about resilience in general but also provides ample clues and opportunities to work on resilience in a practice.

As we elaborated, what predicts whether we are resilient is a certain way of thinking, feeling, and connecting with others. When we take thinking, for example, resilient people are often those that resist black-and-white thinking and leave open the possibility of other perspectives on a certain situation or issue. This is a capability that can be trained, obviously, and the most appropriate place to learn this would be at school or in a related project such as that of the Fort van de Democracy ("Democracy's Fort") discussed in Chapter 9. However, (potentially) vulnerable people might need more than that, and there are several training programs that are designed to fulfill exactly this need. One example is the intervention "Being Muslim Being British," which focuses on developing complexity of thinking to encourage pupils to recognize and accommodate different values at the same time (Liht & Savage, 2013). Another example is the DIAMANT training in the Netherlands, which is featured below in Box 10.6.

Resilience is also more probable when people feel a certain way. When people are able to cope with negative emotions such as anger, frustration, humiliation, and disgust and experience positive emotions such as hope, trust, self-control, and self-esteem, they are more likely to be resilient against radical and extremist messages. Children's social and emotional development is also something that takes place within the confines of the school, but perhaps less so than the cognitive

Box 10.6   Building resilience through the DIAMANT training program

DIAMANT (Diamond; SIPI, 2010) is an example of a training program in the Netherlands run by first-line workers that contributes to the prevention of radicalization through building resilience. It is a three-month training program consisting of three modules focused on, respectively, dealing with a dual identity, intercultural moral judgment, and intercultural conflict management. According to the findings of a thorough evaluation of the program (Feddes, Mann, & Doosje, 2015), the program managed to significantly increase the participants' self-esteem and empathy and their ability to take different perspectives when it comes to analyzing a problem. It thereby seemed to tackle to predictive factors of resilience (thinking and feeling) at the same time.

development. One could think of specific advice and training that help people to cope with negative and emotionally charged events such as experiences of discrimination. Again, programs have been developed to tackle this issue, among them the aforementioned DIAMANT training. Parents also play an important role here, but often need support. Although a combination of parental warmth and a certain degree of control produces the best guarantee for healthy emotional development, many parents struggle to find this balance: they give insufficient support or attention to the child's developing ideals or have problems with setting boundaries – which also has to do with their lack of knowledge about the ideals in question (Sikkens et al., 2018). Elga Sikkens gives the following advice: "Establishing and enforcing limits should be part of the response [to radicalization], but it is more important to teach young people that there are non-violent ways to change society and get one's voice heard" (Sikkens et al., 2018, p. 2283). An important part of stimulating resilience through this emotional dimension should therefore be to provide professional support to parents.

The final predictor of resilience has to do with how we act, and more specifically the way in which we connect with other people. A feeling of connectedness to others and society is important here, as well as specific connectedness to multiple different groups – which, of course, also stimulates positive emotions of trust and the cognitive capacity to recognize different perspectives and truths. This connectedness does not seem to be something that can be realized through training; it is not a capacity, but more a state of affairs. What governments and (to a lesser degree) professionals can do is stimulate these contacts. Youth workers can try to connect different groups of youth in community centers, while teachers can stimulate contact through coupling pupils from different "groups" when making assignment. Governments can play an especially important part by avoiding overly

Box 10.7   Trust in authorities is crucial

In a majority of cases, friends and families were aware of a radicalized individual's plans to carry out a violent act (Gill, Horgan, & Deckert, 2014). The most important reason for not sharing this information with the authorities was a lack of trust in whether the government would get that person in trouble or would help them and fear of potential ramifications from within the community itself (Williams, Horgan, & Evans, 2015).

segregated neighborhoods and through the (stimulation of the) creation of places where diverse people can meet, such as playgrounds, neighborhood centers and schools, or sport clubs.

This final predictive factor of connectedness also shows how resilience can never be only something that is a concern for individuals that may potentially radicalize. To be sure, we mainly focused on individual resilience in this book, partly because the psychological perspective tends to focus on individuals. But it is also – and perhaps especially – families, neighborhoods, schools, and whole societies that need to develop and show resilience if we truly want to prevent radicalization. For communities, for example, this means that internal connections between like-minded people need to be fostered (for a sense of belonging and identity), external connections with people outside the community need to be stimulated (for trust and empathy and against black-and-white thinking), and contacts with the government and other institutions need to be established (for trust and resources that are necessary to address radicalization). And speaking of this latter relationship with the government, it has become clear that the state and municipalities have an important role to play when it comes to building a resilient society. They need to initiate and foster relationships with communities and avoid stigmatizing or prematurely targeting them – as the resulting loss of trust can also spawn more radicalization and may very well seriously impede efforts to detect radicalization in a serious way (see Box 10.7).

Lesson 7: Have a compelling story – and know when to tell it

Radical groups tell a compelling story. It may touch upon needs of friendship and camaraderie, it may trigger the need to be part of something bigger than oneself, or it could just be the weapons and the violence that are appealing. And for some people, the message of a better future and a better world in the form of a bright and shining ideology can be very tempting. For various reasons, radical groups can be attractive for different kinds of people. In a sense, then, radical groups often have a variety of convincing narratives at their disposal (Winter, 2015). Is it possible to counter such a strong narrative?

Not surprisingly, the notion of using counter-narratives as a tool to deradicalize people has become very attractive. The argument that has been put forward is that "we" simply need to feed "them" with the "correct facts" or show appealing alternatives to the terrorist's worldview in order to undermine the claims of radical groups. But is it really that simple?

Unfortunately, we believe it is not. Once people have reached the group membership phase in our model of radicalization, they have become resilient against any attempt to counter their group's narrative (Van Eerten & Doosje, 2019). In that phase, it is not likely that they will pay any attention to such efforts: they only listen to what they want to hear — as most people with strong convictions do. They filter the messages and only process the messages that are in line with their beliefs. Is there a solution?

One option is not to deradicalize people via presenting counter-narratives but to prevent people in the vulnerability phase from reaching the group membership phase. In that phase, people still are open to messages that might contradict the radical group's narrative (Van Eerten et al., 2019). Thus, it is important to have a compelling story to tell, but only as a preventive tool, and not to bank on using this tool in an attempt to deradicalize people.

Lesson 8: Keep doing your job, and do it well

Sometimes preventing (further) radicalization might call for specific types of specialized knowledge and unique interventions. At the same time, this book has shown how the process of radicalization consists of factors that are all too familiar: certain circumstances, events, group-based processes, and basic human needs that we encounter on a daily basis — remember Lesson 1 at the beginning of these chapter. And these factors are often already addressed in existing policies that ultimately target other issues — employment, discrimination, psychological well-being, criminality, addiction — which have inadvertently always contributed to the prevention of radicalization.

Stepping up the fight against radicalization, then, might largely consist of stimulating and intensifying these measures. Similarly, professionals working on the front lines, such as social workers, may very well find radicalization cases to be very similar to cases they normally encounter. That is, at least, what a study showed among such social workers in Norway, who observed that they consider this "business as usual" (Haugstvedt, 2019). Moreover, they indicated that well-established strategies in their line of work, like client-directed practice, Socratic questioning (a form of disciplined questioning that helps to reflect on idea[l]s and assumptions), and motivational interviewing (a nonjudgmental counseling style focused on changing behavior) are also useful in the prevention of radicalization. For a large part, then, preventing radicalization is just a matter of doing one's job — and doing it well.

References

Altier, M. B., Thoroughgood, C. N., & Horgan, J. G. (2014). Turning away from terrorism: Lessons from psychology, sociology, and criminology. *Journal of Peace Research*, 51, 647–661.

Bovenkerk, F. & Vermeulen, F. F. (2012). *Engaging with violent Islamic extremism. Local policies in Western European cities.* The Hague: Eleven International Publishers.

DuBois, D. L. & Alem, F. (2017). *Mentoring and domestic radicalization.* Chicago: National Mentoring Resource Center.

Eijkman, Q. & Roodnat, J. (2017). Beware of branding someone a terrorist: Local professionals on person-specific interventions to counter extremism. *Journal for Deradicalization*, 10, 175–202.

Feddes, A. R., Mann, L., & Doosje, B. (2015). Increasing self-esteem and empathy to prevent violent radicalization: A longitudinal quantitative evaluation of a resilience training focused on adolescents with a dual identity. *Journal of Applied Social Psychology*, 45, 400–411.

Garfinkel, R. (2007). *Personal transformations: Moving from violence to peace.* United States Institute of Peace Special Report 186.

Geurts, R., Granhag, P., Ask, K., & Vrij, A. (2017). Assessing threats of violence: Professional skill or common sense? *Journal of Investigative Psychology and Offender Profiling*, 14, 246–259.

Gill, P., Horgan, J., & Deckert, P. (2014). Bombing alone: Tracing the motivations and antecedent behaviors of lone-actor terrorists. *Journal of Forensic Sciences*, 59, 425–435

Gill, P., Corner, E., McKee, A., Hitchen, P. & Betley, P. (2019). What do closed source data tell us about Lone actor terrorist behavior? *A research note, Terrorism and Political Violence*, 1–18.

Hardy, K. (2018). Comparing theories of radicalisation with countering violent extremism policy. *Journal for Deradicalization*, 15, 76–110.

Haugstvedt, H. (2019). Trusting the Mistrusted: Norwegian Social Workers' Strategies in Preventing Radicalization and Violent Extremism. *Journal for Deradicalization*, 19, 149–184.

Liht, J. & Savage, S. (2013). Preventing violent extremism through value complexity: Being Muslim being British. *Journal of Strategic Security*, 6, 44–66.

Logan, C. & Lloyd, M. (2018). Violent extremism: A comparison of approaches to assessing and managing risk. *Legal and Criminological Psychology*, 24, 141–161.

Sarma, K. M. (2017). Risk assessment and the prevention of radicalization from nonviolence into terrorism. *American Psychologist*, 72, 278–288.

Sieckelinck, S., Sikkens, E., Van San, M., Kotnis, S. & De Winter, M. (2019). Transitional journeys into and out of extremism. A biographical approach. *Studies in Conflict and Terrorism*, 42, 662–682.

Sikkens, E., Van San, M., Sieckelinck, S. & De Winter, M. (2018). Parents' Perspectives on Radicalization: A Qualitative Study. *Journal of Child and Family Studies*, 27, 2276–2284.

SIPI. (2010). *Project DIAMANT: Identiteit, morele oordeelsvorming en conflicthantering [Project Diamond: Identity, moral judgment and conflict management].* Amsterdam: Stichting voor Interculturele Participatie en Integratie.

Stephens, W., Sieckelinck, S. (2019). Working Across Boundaries in Preventing Violent Extremism: Towards a typology for collaborative arrangements. *PVE policy*, 20, 272–313.

Van Eerten, J. J. & Doosje, B. (2019). Challenging extremist views on social media. *Developing a counter-messaging response*. Routledge.

Williams, M. J., Horgan, J. G., & Evans, W. P. (2015). Research summary Lessons from a U. A. study revealing the critical role of "gatekeepers" in public safety networks for countering violent extremism. In A. Zeiger, & A. Aly (Eds.), *Countering violent extremism: Developing an evidence-base for policy and practice* (pp. 139–144). Perth, Western Australia, Australia: Curtin University.

Winter, C. (2015). *'The Virtual 'Caliphate': Understanding Islamic State's Propaganda Strategy*. Quillam Foundation.

Index

Page numbers in *Italic*: Figures; page numbers in **Bold**: Tables